LEADERS ASSEMBLE

LEADERS ASSEMBLE

How to Engage, Transform and Supercharge Your Workforce Through Great Coaching and Leadership

Laura Royal

authors AND CO.

First published in Great Britain in 2024
by Authors & Co.
www.authorsandco.pub

ISBN 978-1-915771-74-2 (paperback)

This book is dedicated to Big Stevie and Wee Ruby
AKA my Mum and Dad.
I am the person I am today because they are a pair of absolute legends.
Thank you for always believing in me.
I love you both hunners (Scottish slang for hundreds).

Contents

About The Author

Who is Laura Royal?

Laura is the owner of DNA Coach, a place where impactful Coaches and Leaders Assemble. As a people and business growth training organisation and consultancy, DNA Coach specialises in all things coaching, leadership, people and culture.

DNA Coach is a Chartered Management Institute (CMI) registered centre providing Level 3, 5 and 7 coaching and leadership qualifications. As a coach training organisation registered with the professional membership body, the Association for Coaching (AC), they provide an accredited Certificate in Coach Training as well as being a recognised CPD training provider of the AC.

Laura is a coach, trainer, public speaker and podcast host with over twenty years in the learning and development space, whilst having also worked internationally for some globally renowned brands, shaping their coaching and learning cultures.

At school, her teachers might have said she talked a little too much and laughed a little too loudly and yet, she has built an entire business, life and career around these two guiding principles – becoming a trainer, coach, consultant and public speaker, as well as being a good human being and someone who has a well-judged sense of humour.

Laura's Obsessions

People

She loves to talk to people, to engage and to support. She will do absolutely anything for her family and friends, especially her parents, Big Stevie and Wee Ruby.

Tea

She recently counted that in one day, she'd drank sixteen cups of tea. She's planning on toning it down to under ten, but she loves a cuppa and even travels with a kettle in the boot of her car.

Dogs

If you are out and about with Laura, then add extra time into your schedule, as she will stop and cuddle all the dogs in the street that she meets. Add more time and gold stars if there is a dog in your home or office. Laura's furry bestie is Tillie, her pride and joy.

Music

If she's not singing (a recovering performer), she'll be listening to all sorts of music. Laura loves karaoke and listening to others sing/perform.

Superhero and Action Movies

Laura loves all the superhero films and watches them on repeat – Terminator 2 is her all-time favourite movie (it's a classic).

Being Warm

Laura hates being cold, she's usually layered up... even when it's only a summer's breeze.

Falling Over

It's not one she goes out of her way to aim for but seemingly it happens often. Laura is quite the calamity queen.

Laughing

As well as a good old chinwag, Laura loves to laugh and finds joy in almost anything. As a fan of a good old joke, her favourite is "What did Batman go to jail for? Robin". It's an oldie but a goodie.

Why is all this random stuff important? Well, it's about knowing the whole person and what makes people tick. You are not solely the person who shows up at work.

At the end of the book, you'll find links to the podcast and some footage of Laura's speaking gigs – some that even involve a wee (Scottish for small or a little) bit of singing and a lot of laughter.

Laura would love it if you'd connect with her on LinkedIn, where she shares more content and musings - **https://www.linkedin.com/in/laura-royal-dna-coach/**

You can check out the DNA Coach website here, **www.dnacoach.co.uk** and find out more about the programmes and services that Laura and the DNA Coach team offer.

Laura and the team provide CMI and AC qualifications and an upcoming CPD membership following the publication of this book. I'd love to work with you.

> You are not solely the person who shows up at work.

DOWNLOAD OUR FREE WORKBOOK THAT ACCOMPANIES THIS BOOK,

IT'S MY GIFT TO SAY THANK YOU!

A Practical Book For Everyone And Anyone In The Workplace

This book was inclusively made for everyone and anyone who works. Even though the premise is about getting *Leaders to Assemble*, it's a read for everyone on what a good workplace should look like, sound like and feel like.

In reading this book you will learn and understand how to:

Unlock and Assemble Your Leadership Superpowers

You'll learn how to tap into your leadership potential and transform the world of workplaces by leading people to be at their best and realise their own potential along the way.

Enhance Your Coaching Skills

Learn practical techniques and strategies through self-coaching opportunities, models and frameworks to become not only a leader but a coach too. This will enable you to support yourself and your team members' growth and development.

Foster Engagement

By implementing the principles shared, you will discover how to create an environment where you and your team members feel motivated, valued and engaged in your workplace.

Drive Transformation

The book will provide insights into leading organisational change and fostering a culture of innovation through making changes and moving forward.

Supercharge Team Performance

Through effective coaching and leadership, you will learn how to unleash the full potential of your people, ultimately by being a good human being and reaping the rewards of increased productivity, creativity and overall performance.

Cultivate a Positive Work Environment

No one wants to work in a shit show. You'll reflect and learn how to continue creating a supportive and inclusive workplace culture where individuals thrive.

Achieve Sustainable Results

Demonstrating what I have shared here, including all of the tools and strategies, you will learn how to achieve long-term success by building resilient teams capable of adapting to change and overcoming challenges.

Develop Personal and Professional Growth

You will not only learn how to lead others but also how to develop yourself as a leader and coach, shaping and influencing continuous growth and improvement in both your personal and professional life.

Inspire Confidence and Trust

Through genuine human-centred leadership and coaching, you will cultivate trust and confidence among team members, encouraging strong relationships built on mutual respect and understanding.

Create Your End Game with Lasting Impact

Ultimately, this book will empower you to become a transformational leader who leaves a lasting legacy, positively impacting everyone throughout your team and the entire organisation.

Each chapter is filled with coaching questions, methods, models (extremely useful to facilitate learning), practices, and things to consider, reflect and act upon. There will be a short Engage, Transform and Supercharge summary at the end of each chapter - some final thoughts, if you will, with the concepts of these grounded throughout each chapter.

Engage

Engaging is about how you build those strong connections and trust and inspire commitment among your team members. It's in how you create an inclusive environment where everyone feels valued, respected and motivated to contribute their best work.

Transform

Transformation lies in how you inspire innovation, challenge the status quo of how things are done and embrace opportunities for growth.

Supercharge

Supercharging represents what you can do to take it up to the next level — going beyond the ordinary to achieve extraordinary results by role modelling and inspiring your people to achieve their full potential.

The Engage, Transform, and Supercharge concepts are far more than just buzzwords —they represent the very DNA of great leadership, organisational growth and people success.

Let's do this.

> No one wants to work in a shit show.

People Stats

Even as a person who genuinely struggles with numbers, I love a little bit of research, ideally, with some data insights to give a flavour of moments in time on how people feel.

Stats and survey data are only a snapshot of the story, but they can play a pretty powerful part in understanding what's going on in an organisation.

Here are a few from some recent articles that I found interesting. It makes me want to go to all of the respondents and ask those companies what they are doing to support their people and create a culture where people can thrive.

Okay, here we go...

FlexJobs surveyed 2,202 people between February 23, 2022, and March 7, 2022, and asked them why they wanted to quit their jobs and how they planned to do it.

The survey of 2,202 workers gave the following five top reasons:

- Toxic company culture (62%)
- Low salary (59%)
- Poor management (56%)
- Lack of healthy work-life boundaries (49%)
- Not allowing remote work (43%)

https://www.flexjobs.com/blog/post/survey-resignation-workers-considering-quitting-jobs/

According to a study conducted by the Ecsell Institute, as reported in a Forbes magazine article by Cara Brennan Allamano,

"Psychological safety in the office leads to more effective communication, better employee retention and increased team performance. Psychological safety also directly impacts the way employees feel about their work and their overall satisfaction: Employees who feel psychologically safe report 76% more engagement, 50% more productivity, 75% less stress and 30% more life satisfaction."

https://www.forbes.com/sites/carabrennanallamano/2023/09/12/human-forward-leadership-how-to-create-a-culture-of-psychological-safety/?sh=f2c29c07a71c

An article on the People Managing People website shares an abundance of stats, with one from Gallup that reported "Companies with engaged employees show better results when compared to those that do not."

Gallup compared business units with high engagement levels with those that don't and came up with the following conclusions. Its employee engagement survey reveals that engaged employees:

- Increase productivity by 14%
- Increase customer ratings by 10%
- Increase sales by 18%
- Increase profitability by 23%
- Increase organisational participation by 13%

https://peoplemanagingpeople.com/culture/employee-engagement-statistics/

You can view the Gallup info here:
https://www.gallup.com/q12/

Imagine the data from the first two I referenced were the results for your business. What would you do? What would be your first step? What would you foresee as an action plan to turn this around so that you have a people-supported culture benefiting from the increased results in the third article's data?

Throughout this book you will learn how to show up and be at your best, in turn, helping others to do the same so that if we did ask your people how they feel at work (and any other fine detail questions about how engaged a colleague is or supported in a psychologically safe way), they would share great feedback that reflects a truly people-focused culture.

If they don't, then there is work to be done. And even if they do, there's always a focus on sustaining that going forward.

Let's get started.

LEADERS ASSEMBLE

Introduction

Leaders Assemble

There has never been a better time, in the world of workplaces, to be people-focused. Therefore, it's time for Leaders to Assemble. If you are an aspiring, new or established leader, this book will take you through the foundations of great leadership and what it means to be, quite simply, a good human being in the workplace.

There has been a big culture shift in organisations.

> People are no longer willing to be micromanaged or to be led by a command-and-control style of management and leadership.

I can't imagine there was ever a time where anyone *liked* that type of environment and even less so now.

You've probably heard of, or even witnessed or experienced, workplace environments that represent 'bums on seats' or where people feel they are just a 'payroll number' or have a 'clock-in and clock-out' approach because they feel like they are merely viewed as a resource and not viewed as the entire person –a human being, complete with a life outside of work; a person with feelings, emotions, expression, individuality and uniqueness. Most, if not all, will have great ideas and want to contribute to the mission and purpose of the business. They want to do great work, to be valued, listened to, appreciated, respected, trusted, empowered and ultimately, to feel safe and supported in the workplace because, let's be honest here, who wants to wake up in the morning, dreading going to work? Nobody. This is why it's essential the culture within a workplace should represent a space where people find security, enjoyment and fulfilment.

> People should be placed at the heart, centre and very core of an organisation because they are the lifeblood and DNA of the business.

It's time that we embrace a people-centred culture in every single workplace, and this can easily be sustainably achieved through great leadership.

Keeping Pace in Our Working World

We all know that the environments we work in have changed considerably since the COVID-19 pandemic, from where we work, to how we work and when we work. How we show up at work has changed too and many of our individual needs, wants, desires and motivations have also shifted.

Long gone are the days when we could leave our home or personal lives at the workplace door. Again, I'm not sure that anyone has truly ever been able to do that but rather, long gone are the days when expressions like that were the norm – it's simply not possible.

Whether you already have a person in your organisation who has responsibility for leading others, such as someone within a supervisory, management or leadership role, or if you are a person who has responsibility for guiding or supporting others in the role of a team buddy, mentor, coach, trainer, people advisor or organisational development professional, or if you are an individual contributor and colleague in the workplace right now, as a worker, but with a keen interest in supporting yourself and others, then this is the book for you.

What Kind of Leader Are You?

What do we mean by the word leadership? Well, the dictionary definition is "The action of leading a group of people or an organisation" but it extends way wider than that. In order to fully understand the definition, I like to check the synonym words. For leadership, we have guidance, direction, authority, control, management, supervision, orchestration and influence, to name a few.

There are a few here that give me the shivers, mainly because my subjective experience of some 'leaders' in the past hasn't always been good. Words like 'authority' and 'control' for example. But there are a few words here that really stand out in a good way - guidance, orchestration and influence.

If we think about the closest synonym, I would say leadership is about influence. Right now, you may not be a 'people leader' or 'manager' but I guarantee you will be leading within other levels and you will be influencing in your everyday interactions.

Think of a time when you have been a leader - not necessarily a leader of a team or department, but a leader in other areas of your life or work. Leadership manifests in a variety of contexts that aren't solely linked to leading at work. You lead every day - in conversation, presentations and decision-making within social groups or with your family, leading the way when you're out and about. There are many examples of everyday leadership.

John C. Maxwell, who wrote *The 21 Irrefutable Laws of Leadership*, said:

"The true measure of leadership is influence, nothing more and nothing less."

Influence isn't about position hierarchy, manipulation or coercion. True influence stems from genuine care for others. Think about the people who have had a positive influence on your life. Now, of course, there will be people who have had a negative influence but what I want you to consider instead is the helpful leadership and ethical influencing qualities that we all possess to help us build better relationships and better environments.

Leading at all levels refers to your ability to demonstrate leadership qualities regardless of your official title or position. Everyone has the potential to lead by example, influence others ethically, and contribute to the collective success of the team or organisation. This approach fosters a culture of empowerment, collaboration and innovation, allowing for a more dynamic and resilient workplace environment.

Beyond Leadership and Management Titles

This book is all about leadership... ethical and authentic leadership, but we often hear the word leadership followed by the word management. You may have a job title that has the word 'manager' attached. I want us to have a flexible mindset when it comes to the words 'leader' and 'manager'.

Of course, there has been a lot written around the concept of 'we lead people and manage things' and I quite like that as a reminder of the nuances and differences of how these roles show up in the workplace and how they are demonstrated by the actions of the people with a role that leads or manages people and things (things here being tasks, functions, projects and departments).

This book is about creating leaders at all levels, regardless of your role right now. It's about positive and helpful influence, how you lead yourself and therefore others, and how you manage yourself, your projects and your workload. Helping you to be the best in all that you do.

I was once given a mug years ago that said:

Positions are temporary... Ranks and titles are limited... But the way you treat people... will always be remembered.

And this has stuck with me. I've tried to find where the quote came from to no avail, it's one of these 'author unknown' quotes but it's one that I really love because it's all about people.

> Regardless of your job title, even the big important fancy ones, you are still a human being on the other side of that job title.

Let's not hide behind them with poor leadership behaviours or autocratic, command and control styles that don't serve your people at its core.

You may have heard the phrase 'people don't leave bad organisations; they leave bad managers', or words to that effect. I truly don't believe this to be the case in all circumstances, but I know a large proportion of people leaving will do so based on things like poor management and leadership practices, a culture that lacks support and development, teams that are led by mini dictators or micro-managers, places where there is little room for growth, advancement, learning or opportunity or businesses where you don't feel included or you don't feel you have a voice that can be shared, heard and listened to. The list is endless.

Beyond your title, good leadership is about role-modelling behaviour. We all have a choice in how we decide to show up and how we interact and engage with others. We can all ensure that our intentions are positive, authentic, sincere and genuine.

Role Modelling

Think of a person who has personally inspired you at work: Note down all of the things about that person that springs to mind such as their style, approach, qualities and attributes. Think about the impact they have had on you as a person. These are all role-modelling qualities, some of which you might even notice exist within you now.

Now bring to mind a person who had the opposite effect on you with their leadership style. Perhaps they completely uninspired you or perhaps they demonstrated an approach and style that you recognised wasn't for you.

This highlights that we all have a choice. We can choose to show up and be great human beings in the workplace and demonstrate an inclusive and engaged style of leadership, or we can demonstrate the opposite with 'bosses behaving badly' in workplaces filled with people dictated to by shitty leaders, ruling and fuelling toxic cultures.

Leaders Assemble

This book is a call to action to create healthy workplace cultures not ruled by fear but instead guided, influenced and curated by people who engage, transform and supercharge workplaces through great coaching and leadership.

Throughout this book, I want you to consider you and your leader within. I want you to consider how you include and engage people through those wonderful role-modelling qualities that you possess. All of those things that make you uniquely you – the authentic you, who doesn't wear a work mask and is a person who effortlessly and ethically influences through great leadership.

In 2023, I held the first Coaches and Leaders Assemble mini-conference in Newcastle, UK, with the ambition of building impactful and inclusive people-centred workplaces. We had speakers who covered multiple topics and we had the objective of helping people be the best in all that they do, both personally and professionally. I want you to be able to help others do exactly the same too and this book is an extension of that ethos, for you to do just that.

A Little Background

I've experienced and observed some really poor cultures in my time, led by some downright shitty and unethical leadership. I've seen leaders who belittle, bully, drive performance through fear, demonstrate toxic behaviours, are demanding and overbearing, unreasonable and unfair. It's this type of leadership that breeds exclusion, unhealthy competition and leaders who would likely describe themselves as assertive and driven when others would view them as aggressive and draining. It's these people, and their behaviours, that build a culture that is not psychologically safe.

It's because of ALL OF THIS, that I do what I do. My ambition is to see a world of workplaces that are people-centred and psychologically safe, underpinned by coaching and great leadership.

I'm certain that's why you are here, too. And this is where we begin, with you. It's about who you are and how you show up. So, who are you from the inside out and the outside in? And what would people say about you in a room you are not in?

It's with this belief, set of values and stance of perspective that I became fully self-employed back in 2016. I'd been working as an organisational development coach with an outsourced consultancy, which gave me a taste of what working on different projects was like and it's where I realised that I had an opportunity to do this for myself.

It's important to stress that, in my twenty-four-plus years of working, I have had some utterly amazing jobs and roles and I have worked for some absolutely wonderful organisations and people. I started my career in the year 2000 in telecommunications as a customer service advisor for a mobile phone operator. I can honestly say, what a time to be alive! It was right at the forefront of mobile technology innovation becoming available to the masses. It was truly a great job and I was bloody good at it.

Where My Leadership Steps Began

Looking back, my leadership journey likely started way back in my performing days, as a singer in bands, as a solo performer and hosting (you might say leading) karaoke events. It's thanks to this that I have an element of comfort in front of an audience, whilst also being a self-professed and proud chatterbox. My school reports always said the same thing – could do better, talks too much, laughs too loud – but here I am, having made a career out of always doing better and talking a lot whilst generally always laughing a lot too.

Have you ever been told you're not smart enough? Me too, and those same people would probably have to pull their chin up off the table if they saw me running my own business now, talking in front of large audiences, sharing ideas and progressing business cultures.

You'll likely remember your own careers talk at school, whether it was in an assembly hall or dusty cupboard room being presented as a *Careers First* hub. They were often mundane, generic and limiting in nature. My 'careers advice' conversation at school went a little something like this: Having responded to the obligatory "What do you want to be when you leave school?" I confidently stated that I wanted to be a vet, only then to be met with a scoff and the statement, word-for-word, "That's not for you, you're not smart enough for that".

Being led to believe that I needed to think smaller was disappointing, to say the least. I can still see young, starry-eyed Laura, being told, "That's not for you" and "You're not smart enough for that", to then being asked what my second choice of career would be. Remembering that I'd watched many LA Law episodes with my parents growing up, and old TV shows like Ironside and Perry Mason, I always loved how the lawyers had a passion for justice and equality and could lead a great debate and dazzle with compelling conversation. I often thought that would be a pretty cool job so I replied to my careers advisor that my second choice would be to become a lawyer. With an eye-roll and another scoff, accompanied by a slap of the pen on the table, the careers advisor took off her glasses and said, "Laura, these choices are way out of your reach.

You'd be far more suited to something a lot less academic. What about beauty therapy or retail or office work?" I didn't question anything, but I did feel stupid, crushed and silly. I had the wind knocked out of my sails. Not only that, but I felt belittled into thinking it was ridiculous that I could even begin to consider being anything like a vet or a lawyer.

Believe it or not, I actually went and got myself a Saturday job as a receptionist in a beauty salon. I absolutely loved it, in all fairness – talking with the customers, selling the skincare and beauty products, watching people come out of their appointment, having had a nice pamper and then going about their day. What I learned in this job is that I really loved engaging with people, helping them and seeing them leave happy. I didn't embark on a career in beauty therapy for no other reason than I don't have the best coordination and did have a practice at doing eyebrow waxing only to then dribble all over the person's face and entire eyebrow. Needless to say, they were not best pleased. Thinking of it now, it does make me giggle.

Where My Passion for a "People" Career Started

A little time later, I applied for a customer service advisor role at One 2 One, as it was known then (which later became T-Mobile and then EE) and started my six-week customer service training. I learned sooooo much in that job; how to communicate effectively, how to resolve complaints, how to deal with complex billing and technology enquiries, how to problem solve and recommend solutions and how to listen for cues and clues to customers' wants and needs, all in a large social environment, in teams, led by some pretty awesome people. I was so good at my job 'on the phones' that I passed my probationary period with flying colours and within six months of being employed, I consistently got 100% call quality for my customer interactions. I moved from a level one advisor, earning £10k per year, to becoming a level three advisor and moving to a £15k salary. I became an internal billing specialist (a billing wizard, as we were known – basically Yoda) and I was loving life. I also helped host some of the social events via my performing background which led to a conversation with the Operations Manager on my interest in becoming a seconded trainer... erm, yes, please!!!!

That's where my career in people started, leading me to become a full-time trainer for our outsourcer and then into various learning, development and coaching opportunities with other businesses, as I was keen to progress. I've worked across varying industries from banking and finance, consumer media, healthcare, automotive, retail and logistics, progressing from training deliverer to head of training and then as an independent consultant from 2016, through to having my own training company.

Throughout all of these positions, I have had some fantastic role models from the likes of Stewart Gemmill, John McElroy, Jessica Kenny (now Higgins), Charlotte Angus, the wonderful Tracey Smith and Alex Underwood to name a few. I'm pretty sure there's something in their approach and style that still lives in me today because I learned from each and every single one of them.

I'm sure if you were to look back across your career path, even as far back as your school careers advice, positive or negative, you could place some links of interest, setbacks and nudges that have shaped and led you to where you are today.

The True Leader Within You

We are all only human, and we don't always get things right. Sometimes we face things, and other times we react as a response. Sometimes, our best self isn't always the one that shows up in the moment. But this is where the sweet spot lies. This is where the learning comes from, through self-awareness and feedback. Being able to share that as human beings we are fallible and can admit our mistakes, and we can work to resolve them, is how we make change and move forward. (You'll hear me mention that turn of phrase a lot in this book).

Wherever you are in your leadership trajectory or path of being a good human being in the workplace (and life too – remember, we're not just the person who shows up at work), let's take a moment to reflect and answer the questions posed:

Who are you from the inside out and the outside in?

Perhaps consider some of your personal core values and beliefs. This may also be a good opportunity to note down your passions and strengths. Maybe even note down the things that you recognise you are good or great at and the things that could do with a wee bit of attention.

What would you want people to say about you in a room that you are not in?

This question helps us consider the intent of our actions and behaviours, that external representation of how you behave, communicate and interact with others, and how this is viewed on the outside. What do other people observe in you? Does it match your internal values and beliefs? Consider some feedback that may have been shared with you.

As you ponder these questions and begin to delve into the depths of your own leadership journey, remember that the true leader within you is not a finished product but rather a work in progress. I'm a big fan of the mantra that we strive for progress, not perfection.

> Embrace the imperfections, the moments of uncertainty and the occasional missteps, for they are all part of the process of growth and development.
> We are only human, after all.

In the chapters that follow, I will help you explore the various aspects of leadership and personal and professional growth, sharing how to navigate the absolute joy of human interaction in the workplace and beyond.

Before we embark on this journey together, I want to leave you with one final thought.

Leadership is not about having all of the answers or being flawless. It's about having the courage to ask the right questions, the humility to learn from your experiences and the resilience to adapt and evolve along the way.

I encourage you to approach it with an open mind, a compassionate heart and a willingness to embrace the journey of becoming the true leader within you.

Together, let's make a change and move forward.

Leaders, let's Assemble!!

THRIVE WITH A TEAM MINDSET

1
THRIVE WITH A TEAM MINDSET

Creating a Culture of Psychological Safety

There is not a single day that goes by where I don't engage in a conversation about Psychological Safety in the workplace. It's something I'm super passionate about and something that you should be super passionate about too. We spend an extraordinary amount of time at work; it needs to be a place where we feel we belong.

One of my biggest values is security, it shows up everywhere in my life. Which is why it was a huge decision for me to become self-employed back in 2016. Taking that security away from a full-time London-based salary while living in Glasgow, where the cost of living is a lot lower, was a massive decision for me. I only had a guarantee for ten days of work at the time, with little-to-no savings that would last me no more than two months.

There was a long list and an accumulation of built-up reasons that led me to make that decision. One is that I wanted to make a difference in the world of workplaces and how people work. Secondly, I was at the point of burnout from being overworked.

I worked for a truly amazing organisation at the time, but I felt exhausted beyond recognition, and I was racking up a lot of hours with a lot of continued weekly travel - so much so that my phone started to recognise the main hotel I stayed in as my home location. Change was needed.

Feeling the pressure to do more and to take on more, I was keen to progress, but I was being given so much that I couldn't fit the work in. Things became 'lunch timey, tea timey, bed timey' projects. Basically, every waking hour projects. Feeling I couldn't say no to some things, I was scared of letting people down or worrying about what they'd think of me if I admitted I was struggling to cope. It's fair to say that at this point in time, I was also going through some quite significant changes in my personal life, too. Poignant as ever to note here, as I said earlier and will continue to say, we are SO much more than solely the person who shows up at work.

The security value for me isn't just about security of income, it's about security of home (the physical location), security of my home life and being there for my loved ones. It's also about feeling safe – safe in my surroundings, safe with the people I am around or I share company with, safe to speak freely, safe to ask questions, safe to say I am stuck on something or I am struggling or I need help, safe to admit I have made a mistake, safe to share ideas or what's on my mind, safe to just be myself and safe to be vulnerable in these "secure" places I spend my time in. And it's this that translates between our home and work environments. And it is this that I wish for you and the people you work alongside, too.

I first came across the phrase the 'psychological contract' early on in my learning and development (L&D) career, when delivering new hire induction and onboarding training. Instantly, it resonated with me pretty much immediately, most likely because the concepts around and within it are shared personal values that are congruent with my own.

The concept of the psychological contract isn't new, in fact, it has been around for decades, since the 1960s, but it seemed to attract more prominence in HR circles within the nineties.

The Chartered Institute of Personnel and Development (CIPD) characterise it well within their factsheet:

The term 'psychological contract' refers to individuals' expectations, beliefs, ambitions and obligations, as perceived by the employer and the worker. It emphasises the importance of the 'human' side to the employment relationship. The psychological contract describes how the parties themselves understand their relationship, their own views of commitment and what they can expect to receive in return.

CIPD go on to outline that:

Broadly, the psychological contract may cover the following aspects of the employment relationship and how they interact:

- *Job security.*
- *Career prospects.*
- *Training and development.*
- *Perceived fairness of pay and benefits.*
- *Manager support.*
- *Employer's contribution and impact on communities and society.*

So, even without having yet delved into psychological safety, we can see that the unwritten (in comparison to an official employee contract outlining T&C's) and implicit expectations, along with perceptions that people have about reciprocal obligations and treatment in the workplace, aren't new, and from my perspective, are more than reasonable.

Let's strip it back to the core once again. Remember, it's about being a human being in the workplace and being treated like a human being in return.

Too often, I have come across entire cultures and micro 'in team' cultures displaying command and control style approaches... ones that can be likened to our schooling. Typically, these unhelpful cultures are led by or include people role-modelling toxic behaviours.

One of the greatest organisational practices that will ensure your entire workplace is one where people thrive, is that of psychological safety. Keep in mind all of the wonderful things that a psychological contract brings and take it to version 2.0. That's what psychological safety is.

Psychological safety isn't a new concept either, it's steeped in vast history and iterations that we can track right back to the work of Abraham Maslow, and the Hierarchy of Needs. As far back as the 1940s and through to the key work of Carl Rogers in the 1950s and the work of Edgar Schein and Warren Bennis, psychological safety is referenced. Further work was done by William Kahn and Amy Edmondson in the late nineties into the noughties Amy continues to be a key thought leader and researcher in this field. More recently, Timothy Clark expanded on research with the Four Stages of Psychological Safety in 2020.

I've heard a fair amount of pushback from people when talking about psychological safety, saying that it was the latest business speak or buzzword or phrase that came out of the pandemic. I can safely say that this is not the case, but what the pandemic did aid in that sense was a recognition that workplace cultures had shifted further away from the strict authority of command-and-control approaches and more positively towards people-centred cultures and practices, particularly around flexibility, resilience, engagement and well-being at work.

Let's look at a few definitions of what psychological safety is.

Timothy Clark neatly outlines this definition:

"Psychological safety is a condition in which you feel ***1 - included, 2 - safe to learn, 3 - safe to contribute and 4 - safe to challenge the status quo****, all without fear of*

being embarrassed, marginalised or punished in some way."

Amy Edmondson states that psychological safety is:

"The belief that one will not be punished or humiliated for speaking up with ideas, questions, concerns or mistakes, and the team is safe for interpersonal risk-taking."

Whilst I absolutely love these definitions (and also being a huge fan girl of Amy and Timothy's work), I like to strip it right back.

Think of a short enough statement that we could sew onto a pillow today and sell on Etsy - a Live Laugh Love of psychological safety, if you will... are you ready?

Don't be an asshat at work.

Asshat (noun) is a colloquial term used to describe someone who behaves foolishly, obnoxiously or inconsiderately.

There, I said it, in print (I often say this out loud). There are a few other variations that you can come up with yourself as well, I'm sure.

Beyond the fundamental definitions, it's about what you do and how you make people feel, showing up at work and being a good human being. It's about leaving any ego at the door, not shooting anyone down, ridiculing or embarrassing them. It's about embracing our authenticity without fear of judgement, reprisal or any negative consequence.

I genuinely feel that most (if not all) people don't get up in the morning and think to themselves, "I'm going to go in and ruin everyone's day today at work by being shitty", but that doesn't mean that we can't look to approach things in a more human and thoughtful way that seeks to draw the best out of our people, the best outcomes for our teams and a sizable impact within our workplace cultures.

My lovely friend, Jack Williamson, published his book, 'The Shitty Committee', which is a no-punches-pulled, generation-defining go-to guide for anyone who is ready to stop feeling like shit and start living a more fulfilling life. If that's you, then read on and read his book – but read this one first, though. The title of his book has stuck with me over the last few years, as I think about people demonstrating a lack of psychological safety as being part of a Shitty Committee in the workplace – and we definitely don't need those individuals leading our organisations.

An important distinction to make here is when you think of the average working week. With the average being forty hours, it should be time well spent rather than feeling it's time served. We should all feel safe, secure and supported at work.

So how does a lack of psychological safety show up in the workplace? What does that look like, feel like or sound like? And in comparison, what would a culture of psychological safety look, feel or sound like?

Take this quick self-assessment, answering with a Yes, No or Sometimes. Go with your immediate response and don't overthink it.

- Do you feel comfortable speaking up in meetings or sharing your ideas without fear of negative repercussions?
- When you make a mistake, do you feel supported and encouraged to learn from it?
- Are you able to ask questions or seek clarification without worrying about appearing incompetent or being judged?
- Do you feel like you can be your regular, everyday self at work?
- Do you feel like your contributions are sought out, valued and recognised?
- Are there clear channels for communication and feedback within your organisation?
- Do you feel a sense of connection and belonging in your team or workplace overall? (Note that your responses to this may differ.)
- Overall, do you feel psychologically safe at work?

Ultimately, psychologically safe environments will attract quick-fire 'yes' responses. Cultures where psychological safety is not present will attract huge volumes of 'no' responses. Cultures where there is a lack of consistency will lead people to choose a 'sometimes' response, also identifying a culture lacking in psychological safety.

You can use a five or seven-point or a standard ten-scaled system and measure this all day long but a smaller scale reacting survey for a quick culture assessment can be hugely powerful.

If you answered 'sometimes' or 'no' to any of those questions, this is a sign that there is work to do.

Let's not get complacent, either. If you answered 'yes' to any of the questions (which is what we are striving for) then there is continued work to do to remain consistent.

A culture that's engaged, on the pulse or using words like psychological safety isn't the thing to simply hang your hat on though. It's the strides we take in order to live and breathe a culture of psychological safety every single day that makes the difference.

Dolly Parton sang about the world of workplaces in her 1980s song 9 to 5. Little did we realise that Dolly was talking about a culture that lacked psychological safety. Well, officially, 9 to 5 is the title song to the film of the same name, which highlighted gender inequality in the workplace, but the lyrics fit well for psychological safety overall, too.

Let's have a little singalong in your mind by singing the opening verse of 9 to 5 up to and including the chorus. Do it out loud if you want to of course. And if you have never heard the song before then get it open on YouTube full volume.

Dolly is singing that her workplace feels like it's all about what can be taken from you, leaving her feeling no more significant than an anonymous cog in a machine or just another number on the payroll. The creativity and hard work poured into the job seem to vanish into thin air, with not even a word of appreciation in return. That certainly doesn't sound psychologically safe now does it.

I delivered a talk on this very subject at my very own Coaches and Leaders Assemble Conference in Newcastle UK in June 2023. Yes, you can sing along in your own mind if you're not already, but the lyrics hit a point.

Not only do I want you to think about NOT being an asshat at work and not being part of (or leading) the shitty committee but also, I want you to cultivate a truly people-centred workplace culture so that 'folks like me' (and you and everyone else) on the job can work a more fulfilling NINE to THRIVE (see what I did there?).

You can even watch a wee video of me leading a singalong with that very song at the conference here - www.dnacoach.co.uk/9tothrivesingalong

Think about the kind of things that prevent you from feeling psychologically safe at work.

Even take it back to the foundations: what about your workplace causes you to feel uneasy, unhappy, disengaged or discontent? What fuels a feeling of exclusion in your workplace?

Think about some of the times when you may feel vulnerable in the workplace, perhaps when you got something wrong. Ask yourself what prevents you from feeling safe to say to someone, 'I've made a mistake', 'I'm feeling stuck here', or 'I need help'? What stops you from asking questions when you don't know something or if you want clarity or more information?

Think about any time you may have had a concern about something you've felt, observed or experienced. What stopped you from speaking up and highlighting it?

Have there been times you had a different opinion on something or a different idea, perhaps even a disagreement with another person? If you answered yes, but you didn't open up a conversation about it, what stopped you? What made you decide to remain silent?

Have you ever thought to yourself, "I've got an idea that would really help here, one that would mean that something would have to change in order to improve or enhance something that we do around here"? Did you share that with your colleagues, leaders or managers? If not, what stopped you from bringing that idea to the table?

Even if the responses to the above feel like teeny tiny examples, note them down and then ask yourself how often or how frequently this is showing up. When does this happen? Who is around (or not around) when I experience this? Where is it happening?

These are some of the questions I ask individuals and teams to explore to really identify the everyday things that prevent them from feeling that sense of belonging and safety in the workplace. When I run my programme on how to THRIVE with a team mindset, which is all about psychological safety and inclusion within the workplace, this is what we discuss and ask ourselves.

The responses always vary in scale, magnitude and impact.

People report they feel scared to speak up because of experiences they've had in the past (sometimes the very recent past) where feedback from others and their responses to these questions from those situations could be ones of limiting beliefs and judgement.

Some open examples of having team members or 'bosses behaving badly' with poor behaviours presented themselves. It's common to hear examples of people who would identify themselves as 'assertive' but actually, their behaviour just comes across as direct, rude, borderline aggressive, demanding, overbearing or quite simply, mean and shitty. This dilutes everyone's confidence to speak up, engage and contribute.

In these situations, we are stifling creativity and innovation, creating cultures that hold people back or impact a person's self-worth, value and potentially, their well-being.

I often hear examples of more severe behaviours of bullying, harassment and victimisation with blame and finger-pointing at the core, where people 'wallpaper their backside' to protect their shortcomings, perhaps by positioning blame elsewhere.

Here's a long list (not an exhaustive one) of examples that people share in responses to the things we've experienced before that prevent us from feeling psychologically safe at work:

- Geographical splits due to remote and hybrid working
- Not being invited to meetings, events, lunches etc.
- Information not being shared (either at all, or not frequently enough, missing information, or only shared in certain circles and not being updated after absences)
- Feeling ignored or dismissed
- Being talked over and feeling their voice is suppressed
- Team cliques and team divides
- Lack of diversity and inclusion
- Not being asked for contributions, thoughts, ideas, feedback or suggestions
- Lack of both formal and informal recognition
- Not feeling valued and feeling that their efforts go unnoticed

- Feeling that others in the team have more to say or offer
- Feeling that diverse viewpoints are unwelcomed
- Constantly being shut down or feeling that only certain voices are entertained
- Given a lack of time and resources, perpetuating the feeling of overwhelm and of being overworked
- Given little or no opportunity for development
- Witnessing favouritism and workplace bias
- Fearing reprisal, repercussions or being made to look stupid (sensing the risk and worry if a mistake is made)
- Sensing a culture of blame and punishment (an ‘it wasn’t me’ type of culture)
- Negative consequences
- Seeing a lack of innovation and creativity
- Micromanaging or dictating cultures
- Feeling that speaking up is a waste of time and energy
- Worrying that discussion results in conflict
- An unhealthy or inappropriate challenge towards others
- Being actively discouraged from contributing
- Viewing disagreements or dissent as trouble-making
- Unhelpful hierarchy, particularly ego-driven ones
- People's attitudes to styles and personalities
- Toxic manifestation of behaviours and expressions
- Being overworked and under-resourced
- Feeling underrepresented
- Having to take work home

- Unrealistic expectations being set

We hear many examples in the media - more often than we should - of toxic workplace cultures leading to severe and devastating outcomes where lives are tragically lost. This all links back to people not feeling psychologically safe in speaking up if something isn't right, for fear of reprisal or repercussion.

Let that sink in for a minute - lives lost due to the prevailing culture in an organisation being led by people actively being an asshat.

Now, of course, that is an extreme example to illustrate just how far a lack of psychological safety can go, but all of this needs to be turned around.

I genuinely don't think that (most) people wake up on any given day and decide to go into disruptive mode to ruin everyone else's day or to cause a ruckus or even to be an asshat, BUT, the key word here is 'decide'. We all have a choice in how we want to show up at work, how we choose to behave, how we choose to engage with others, how we decide to lead, how we include others and how we decide to contribute. Most folks wake up with the intention of being a good human being, doing their best by themselves and supporting others to foster and positively shape the environments and the spaces that we take up. We want to create workplaces that people want to be in. We also have a choice in being able to craft these environments where everyone feels included, valued, supported, empowered and championed. These are the places that we want to be in and that enable us to thrive.

So, let's turn it around, now!

The answers you consider to my next question may be the complete opposite to everything mentioned before but this is where we should spend more time thinking about exactly what that looks like, what that sounds like and what that feels like. We should even be able to smell it in the air and taste it to the point where it's palpable.

It's now time to think about the kind of things that ensure you feel Psychologically Safe at work.

Once again, let's take it back to the foundational building blocks and ask what about your workplace causes you to feel at ease, happy, engaged and content.

Consider the definitions shared earlier around inclusion. What fuels a feeling of inclusion in your workplace?

Think about the times when you have felt that you belonged, where you felt that you fit in, where people had your back, where you felt supported, able to pose ideas and suggestions, to ask questions (even the ones where you felt a hesitation in yourself for whatever reason), where maybe you got things wrong but you could develop yourself along with being able to progress and had the confidence to speak up. What (and who) aided all of that? What environment are you in within those moments? Who else is there? How are all of these things coming across and how are they manifesting in the behaviour of others?

Consider what it is about your workplace that makes it enjoyable. What are the everyday things that people do that make you feel safe and that you belong? What are the big and small actions of others that support that environment?

Note everything down that springs to mind here. Like before, even if any of the responses to the above only feel like teeny tiny examples, note them down and list them out. And then ask, how often or how frequent is this showing up? When does this happen? Who is around (or not around) when you experience this? Where is it happening?

Because I don't know about you… no, actually, I do know about you because you are here, reading this book, which means that YOU care about people.

I know that this is the environment we all want to be in every working day. The one where we 'Do a Dolly' and know that working nine to five (or whatever your core hours are) is a way to make a living.

Here's another lovely long list (not an exhaustive one) of examples that people share in response to the things we've experienced before and that helps people feel psychologically safe at work:

- Taking an interest in the whole person, not just the person that shows up at work
- People know your name and you are known to others

- A workspace where you can speak openly and freely
- Thoughts and feedback are welcomed and sought out
- You can be yourself and all of the wonderful things that make you uniquely you
- Learning and development, both personally and professionally, is taken seriously
- You feel 'invested in' as a person and not just a resource
- You have the ability to progress
- You have some say or autonomy over what you do and how you do it
- You feel trusted and empowered to act as well as to contribute
- People check in on your well-being and workload
- You feel updated and communicated with
- You feel part of something with purpose
- You feel recognised for your efforts as well as progress, success and achievements
- You feel supported when you need help or if you have made a mistake
- You feel resilient and able to deal with the day-to-day
- There are opportunities for growth and potential is championed
- There is a strong sense of camaraderie
- You feel a part of a team and have a sense of belonging
- Diversity of self, thought, perspective and background is celebrated

- Well-being is a priority and you feel looked after and looked out for
- Opinions are sought after
- Feedback is a two-way conversation as a minimum
- People role model great behaviours
- Open communication thrives and people are approachable
- Being listened to, along with being treated with kindness and respect is a given
- You feel accepted and welcomed
- You feel warmth from others
- You feel connected and engaged
- You are also surrounded by other good human beings
- You are fairly and equitably treated as a person and not only in terms of remuneration
- You experience good workplace conditions and offerings
- And finally, a work-life balance is supported.

> Every single person in the workplace should feel included regardless of what they look like, how they sound, who they love, where they live or what their background is.

I could get on my soapbox further about this topic and literally talk about it the whole day long (and maybe this entire topic will be book number two, who knows) but you get the gist of it for now.

Taking the above list, let's take a critical review of it and acknowledge that all of these points are within the reach of every single one of us. We are all capable of this. It's a given choice. A decision to act.

As leaders, managers, organisations and people, let's do right by the individuals that make up our businesses because they are the DNA and very fabric of your company. Because when one person thrives, we can all thrive too.

Mindful Micro Expressions

We must be mindful to consciously check in on ourselves and consider micro-expressions, our choice of words, how we convey our words, our intent, our manner, our style and our approach.

What do I mean by micro expressions? Micro expressions are fleeting facial expressions that occur within a fraction of a second, often revealing an emotion or reaction. We're all familiar with them, we even use them as emojis – just think how many times you've sent an eye roll emoji to a friend.

Microexpressions shut down a person's interactions or contributions. Consider this example: You're in a team meeting, hearing about a business update and there's the opportunity to ask a question. You are uncertain of key aspects of what's been shared and build the confidence to ask something or perhaps even share a concern and it's met with an eye roll from a team member. How would that make you feel? Probably less likely to ask a question or raise a concern the next time because it fuels a feeling that we shouldn't have asked a question in the first place. We then start to second guess what people are thinking of us at that moment.

Here's a couple I am sure you are familiar with:

The eye roll - this typically indicates contempt, annoyance or disbelief.

A curl of the lip - this can signify disregard or disdain.

A nose wrinkle - this often indicates a dislike.

A furrowed eyebrow - this can signal confusion, concentration or concern. I often got told off in school for 'scowling' because I had a furrowed brow, but this is genuinely my go-to concentration facial expression, so it's important not to assume.

An eyebrow raise - a raise of the eyebrows can signify surprise, interest or scepticism.

Sometimes these reactions are so spontaneous and may not be meant to cause a person to feel stupid or anxious or to intentionally undermine, so, in these moments, it's helpful to meet it with acknowledgement and to invite a conversation with something along the lines of "*I noticed there was a reaction there, talk to me about your thoughts on that*".

We should feel safe to hold these conversations in a respectful way, tactfully, professionally and conversationally.

Remember, demonstrating psychological safety is a choice. We all have a choice in how we show up and choose to interact with others.

We also need to call out behaviours that are not psychologically safe and not make excuses for people's poor behavioural decisions. For example, I have often heard phrases like: "Oh, don't take any notice of them, that's just their style, they don't mean any harm" or "That's just who or how they are, take it with a pinch of salt" or even "Don't worry, they're like that with everyone, it's not just you."

No, nope, none of that is ok. Let's open up a discussion with them about it and share how that style or approach makes us feel and the impact that has on us.

This is where we can all practise psychological safety by intentionally choosing our actions and behaviours. It's not only reserved as something that a person with a more nurturing or warm personality style can demonstrate.

Psychological Safety is NOT a Personality Factor

It's not solely determined by individual personalities but rather by the culture, dynamics and modelling behaviour within that group. While individual personalities certainly play a role in how comfortable someone may feel about speaking, psychological safety is largely influenced by the group environment and team approach. Factors such as leadership style, team norms, communication structures and organisational culture all contribute to the level of psychological safety within a team or group setting.

THRIVE with a Team Mindset

We know that psychological safety plays an important role in well-being and therefore, it is important that our workplace environments allow a safe place for us all to manage change and uncertainty, to speak freely and to have an effective voice within our organisations. It is important to reflect that we are all included within a culture of team cohesion and team spirit while also meeting our innate needs to learn, grow and thrive.

So, let me introduce you to the THRIVE with a Team Mindset™ model.

Firstly, what do we mean by the word THRIVE? Put quite simply, this is an opportunity to grow, prosper and flourish. You can use the word THRIVE to guide your psychological safety practices. I have created it as a handy mnemonic with some definitions along with some coaching questions to prompt conversation, awareness and action.

Trust and Team

For psychological safety to be present, we must ensure that a strong foundation of trust is in place and that there is a strong sense of team spirit and mindset evident.

There is a clear distinction between psychological safety and trust. They are linked, of course – trust amongst your team members, colleagues and leaders contributes to having a psychologically safe culture and without it, we breed a culture of division and exclusion.

Trust brings the team together. Teaming is where we team up to achieve a common goal, where we join forces to collaborate and where we get together. Trust helps us to then bind this all together.

Ask yourself:

- How can you build trust at work?
- How well are you listening to your people and seeking their ideas, suggestions and opinions?
- How confident do your people feel that no one on the team will embarrass or punish anyone else for

admitting a mistake, asking a question or offering a new idea?

- How do you embody team spirit in a way that helps your people bond with their colleagues?
- How do you encourage collaboration, teamwork and high levels of team spirit? How is team spirit modelled at the director and executive level?
- How will you make it easy for people to share ideas and concerns, and worry less about hierarchy or what people will think of each other?
- How will you build a culture where teaming is the norm? How will you help everyone to become curious, passionate and empathic?

Happy and Human

Let's be honest, no one wants to be unhappy at work – it's where we spend a large chunk of our time. We are also not a number or a robot and as such, don't want to be made to feel like one. To cultivate psychological safety, we should strive to make work a more happy and more human experience.

Be curious about the people you work with, know yourself and your team members and take a genuine interest in the life and work of your colleagues. Be able to express your gratitude to the people around you and encourage your team to not be afraid to show up as their true selves at work.

Talk with your team members regularly, find out what people care about, what they want and what support you can offer.

Think about these questions:

- How will you get to know your teammates, what they bring to the team and how they can contribute?
- What are the strengths of each team member and how can you use these to provide the best support to your people?
- What is important to each team member about their work? What does this mean for the way that you work with them?
- How will you show that you want to know your team well and work with them better?
- How do your people know that you care for them?
- How do you create a workplace that supports its team members' personal needs at all levels of the business?
- How do you meaningfully connect with yourself and others? What does that look, sound and feel like?

Respect and Recognise

It's important to encourage mutual respect in your workplace, even when people may disagree with one another. This should be a place where the truth can be spoken and where there is an abundance of respect. In knowing this, we feel the comfort of being safe within that space. When respect is evident, people feel safe to be themselves and express their ideas and that comes from a place of being happy and feeling secure.

Recognition plays a huge part in psychological safety too. When team members' efforts are recognised, and people feel appreciated, there are higher levels of morale, motivation and engagement with ultimately discretionary effort. And it will be of no surprise then that when we cultivate respect and recognition, this can also strengthen the trust we have across our teams.

Knowing your team well and having greater social awareness alongside great relationship management can aid you in knowing exactly how each team member would prefer to be recognised. It's not a one-size-fits-all affair and people will respond to recognition in a variety of different ways.

Here are some coaching questions to prompt conversation, awareness and action:

- How can you encourage mutual respect at work?
- How do you know that your team members feel respected? What should you do if you observe disrespectful behaviour?
- How will you establish and reinforce an authentic, consistent foundation of respect for all of your team members?
- How do you recognise your team members in a personal way? In what ways are you recognising your people?

- How will you create a meaningful recognition culture? How do team members know that their contribution is valued?
- How do you recognise major accomplishments as well as the smaller, everyday efforts?
- How do you share meaningful gestures of gratitude? How can you boost peer-to-peer recognition?
- How do you recognise efforts in a way that lives up to the expectations of your people? How will you constantly re-evaluate the rewards and recognition efforts of your organisation?

Invite and Include

We need to invite participation, invite feedback, invite collaboration and extend this invitation to every single member of the team, every single day, during every single interaction. Only when we do this can we have true inclusion.

The need to feel a sense of belonging will be familiar to us all. This fundamental principle ensures that psychological safety is present by making certain that no one is left out/or behind and that everyone is included. This goes further by also making sure that your people are included in important discussions and decisions whilst also importantly considering how you communicate and encourage active participation within discussions. Your team members should feel accepted for who they are and valued for what they bring.

Reflect and think about:

- How are you building a culture where everyone feels included? What does inclusion look like in practice?
- What conscious and unconscious bias may be present in your team? How can you create a shift from any unconscious bias to conscious inclusion?
- How can you build a more inclusive workplace? How do you accept people for who they are and value them for what they can bring to the team?
- How important is it to you to feel like you belong and that people in your team are loyal?
- How do you react when you feel rejected? How can you ensure this is not present in your team?
- How do you meaningfully connect with yourself and others? What does that look, sound, and feel like?
- How do you interact with the team and how do you take a genuine interest in them and build relationships with your colleagues?
- How is your business fostering connections amongst your people?
- How can you generate a culture of good communication? How can you create more opportunities for effective communication?

Value and Voice

As a leader in your business, you should understand the importance of your people, the value they offer and the value you should demonstrate for their efforts and contribution. Every single person's voice in your team has value and it's important that it is listened to. How well do you live and breathe the values of your organisation and how does this align with your personal values? How are you then meeting these values for your team members?

We can link the opportunity for team member contribution here by considering how free your team members are to offer ideas and suggestions, to come up with new ways of working or innovative practices. We can also link this by asking how safe is it for your team members to challenge the ways things are typically done with the betterment of the team and organisation in mind. There are opportunities here for your organisation to grow by encouraging team members to actively take part in creating value without being forced – a place where creativity and innovation are welcomed.

Reflect and consider:

- How will you tap into the values your people possess and uncover core values that link to your team and organisation values?
- What do you value? What unspoken values have contributed to your team's successes to date?
- What values do your team members have in common? What values should overarch the way you interact with each other and with customers?
- What do your team values mean to you? What does it look like in action? How will you integrate

these values into everyday practice? How will you evaluate adherence to it?

- How will it change or strengthen your relationships and interactions?
- How will you create a workplace where every voice matters? How will you encourage people to speak up?
- How will you encourage team members to share their voices? How will you shape and foster an environment where people are able to speak up without fear of rejection or ridicule?
- How will you adopt behaviours and practices that support effective voices and embed this at all levels?
- How will you provide formal and informal opportunities through which real dialogue, individual and collective, can take place?
- How much say do your team members have in your business and overall, how well does this work?

Engage and Empower

It is so important to ensure, when working with your team, that you engage with the whole person, their hearts and minds, to establish a culture where safety is present, and where we have great engagement that consistently leads to positive business results.

The engagement of your team and the individuals within it isn't something that should only be measured on an annual survey. It needs to be at the core of everything you do. Engagement drives behaviour and performance. As well as giving your people a voice, they need to be heard. Taking time to engage with each person and elicit feedback on what's working well and what's not, can be really powerful. Encouraging a collaborative approach to feedback can be a real impactful driver of engagement.

Our workplace conversations should be ones that empower people to make changes and move forward, to take interpersonal risks with the support of your team members and leaders. You have a real opportunity to engage and encourage people to reach their optimum potential.

Take a moment and ask yourself:

- What do you like about your role, your team and your company? What do you dislike? What can the business do more/less of?
- What would be helpful for you and your people? What would help strengthen engagement?
- What can your manager/leader/colleague do to help? How will you support personal and professional well-being?
- How do you empower yourself and your people? How do you foster autonomy to help people flourish?
- How will you help team members feel more comfortable developing as professionals in your company? How do you provide support for them to feel confident in their roles?

- How will you allow your people to take leadership of their roles? What high impact and positive long-term effects could this bring?
- How will you invest in empowerment within your workplace?

There has never been a more important time than now to focus on the well-being of your people and the success of your business. I want your people and your business to THRIVE during these uncertain times, and beyond, and that starts with you. It's your responsibility as a great leader, colleague and human to look after the safety and well-being of your team members.

Everyday Things That Truly Help People to Feel Psychologically Safe

- Remembering not to be an Asshat is always first and foremost, closely followed by helping other people to also not be an Asshat.
- Actively and actually truly listen when you ask your people how they are doing.
- Offer genuine help and support – be approachable. This is a big differentiator: you're checking in, not checking up on people.
- Demonstrate your gratitude for the person, their work and their effort.
- Continually ask people what they think and encourage the sharing of ideas, comments and suggestions.
- Invite people to come up with new and even wild ideas – this encourages creativity, collaboration and innovation.
- Go and have that cuppa with a colleague: find out more about them inside and outside of work.
- Don't put people on the spot but invite feedback in a way that a person is comfortable contributing.
- Consider what you want to convey; how best can you share that in a helpful way?

Engage, Transform, Supercharge 'Psychological Safety' Summary

Engage

When we start exploring psychological safety in our workplace, it's like turning on a light bulb in a dark room. We gather everyone around, share stories and talk about what it means to feel safe and supported at work. We're not just ticking boxes; we're building understanding and trust. We show how being open, honest and respectful with each other can make a world of difference. It's about creating an environment where everyone feels valued and heard, where we can all be ourselves without fear of judgement or criticism. Together, we're laying the foundation for a workplace where people can thrive.

Transform

As we dive deeper into the idea of psychological safety, we're really focusing on making it a part of who we are and how we work. It's not just about saying the right things; it's about living them every day. We lead by example, showing vulnerability, empathy and kindness in everything we do. We're creating spaces where people feel safe to speak up, share ideas and take risks. We're breaking down barriers and building bridges, connecting people and ideas in new and exciting ways. This isn't just about change; it's about transformation – for us, our teams and our organisation.

Supercharge

We're taking things to the next level, together. We're not just talking about psychological safety; we're living and breathing it in everything we do. We're embedding it into the very foundation of our organisation because it's in our DNA and it's in yours, too, from your values and mission to your day-to-day practices and policies. We're measuring our progress, gathering feedback and celebrating successes along the way, but we're not stopping there. We're always looking for new ways to supercharge psychological safety, to make our workplace even better for everyone. Because when we feel safe and supported, there's no limit to what we can achieve together.

Small Steps Make Big Leaps

Let's Not Stop Here: keep the momentum going and refer to the THRIVE Toolkit section in your downloadable workbook. Share it with your team and use this as an action plan to work on together.

www.dnacoach.co.uk/leadersassembleworkbook

TUNE IN, TURN ON BUT DON'T COP OUT

2

TUNE IN, TURN ON BUT DON'T COP OUT

Leading With Emotional Intelligence

Something that goes hand-in-hand with psychological safety is *Emotional Intelligence*, so it feels right and perfectly placed to share more on this subject at this stage in the book.

I first heard about emotional intelligence around 2006, when taking on my first proper leadership role in learning and development. All of a sudden, I was thrown into meetings with people with big, fancy, capitalised job titles – head of this or director of that. I remember one particular meeting hadn't gone particularly well. A systems implementation delay held back the launch date for a client, which therefore held back the recruitment of people and therefore the training plan. The knock-on effect of this delay was potentially huge. It was the first time I properly realised that there are so many moving parts to things.

Perhaps being a little naïve, I had previously just focused on my area and not all of the component pieces of the jigsaw that had to be put into place before I had a room of twelve new hire team members to train, but I was a manager now; my role had become more strategic, and less delivery focused. It was very exciting to be involved in something brand new for a client (I was working for an outsourced operational call centre for a large telecoms and media client). I was eager to absorb all of the learnings and to put this all into practice to deliver an outstanding service.

It was in this meeting (where essentially, the shit metaphorically hit the fan) that I first heard the phrase shared that someone lacked emotional intelligence because they couldn't 'read the room'. They didn't understand the variety of perspectives and hadn't paid attention to what someone else was trying to say and instead had an outburst and made rash decisions without considering the wider impact on the people involved.

Having asked my colleagues what emotional intelligence was, they gave a few statements on various things which ended with a powerful metaphor which has stuck with me ever since. They said *it was like being able to see the view from another person's hilltop.*

> See the view from another person's hilltop.

Now, of course, it's that and so many other things but I live by this so much. It's that nice link to empathy (which is a key part of emotional intelligence, too) that for me is an extension of walking a mile in another person's shoes. Because it's then, and only then, that you can understand what it's like from another person's multi-layered point of view.

Several metaphoric examples have popped up along the way and many have sprung to my mind over the years on which further describe emotional intelligence. You'll see the thread of them throughout this book as I use models, themes and metaphors jointly alongside mnemonics to explain things that have helped me remember stuff over the years.

One metaphor that I've always quite liked in describing emotional intelligence is to imagine it as a compass that might guide us through the sunshine and storms of the emotions we feel and express. We use the compass as a guide to our destination.

Another favourite is to visualise it as being a key to unlocking doors to meaningful relationships by knowing our own emotions and understanding the emotions of others.

Described by Experts: What Exactly is Emotional Intelligence?

Following the meeting where another person was described as lacking in emotional intelligence, I directed myself towards Borders Books in Glasgow and bought Daniel Goleman's book, *Emotional Intelligence*. I still have the exact copy, all yellow and tatty now but what a great book, albeit quite heavy going for me at the time. It was this very book that led me to learn more about the inner workings of the brain. I was (and still am) fascinated by its depths.

The book described and discussed our IQ (intelligence quotient) and highlighted that it wasn't the be-all and end-all that I was led to believe it was in school. If you remember in my previous chapter, you'll recall I was told I wasn't 'smart enough' to become a vet or a lawyer and whilst those aspirational roles no longer applied to me, the pain of those limiting words had burned for a long time as truth in my head. Goleman's book acted as an epiphany moment for me. It was at this time that I also discovered the power of our mindset. Of course, we now know even more about the power of a growth mindset these days, which we will come to later in the book. So yes, IQ is one thing but then there is EQ, our Emotional Quotient, and this can be strengthened and nurtured in all of us.

One of the simplest definitions of emotional intelligence that Goleman shares in this book is that "*Emotional intelligence is being able to rein in emotional impulse, to read another's innermost feelings, to handle relationships smoothly*".

Utterly brilliant – once again, it's about being a good human being. This really shouldn't be so hard, should it? But sometimes, for some people, it is.

In his book, Goleman shares how being emotionally intelligent can strengthen relationships and a lack of it can corrode them with toxic emotions, putting our physical health at as much risk as chain-smoking (quite a bold statement in the mid-nineties when this book was published) and that emotional balance can help protect our health and wellbeing.

His later work goes on to outline five key components or domains of emotional intelligence, with these being self-awareness, self-regulation, motivation, empathy, and social skills. This was reworked again later in his work with four domains being that of self-awareness, self-management, social awareness and relationship management.

The four domains of emotional intelligence are also the ones that are referred to in the work of Jean Greaves and Travis Bradberry in their book, Emotional Intelligence 2.0, which is again, an outstanding read that I would highly recommend if you want to delve deeper into the subject.

Let's use this simple definition of what emotional intelligence is to guide us, along with the definitions of each domain and some questions to consider:

Emotional intelligence is the ability to understand and manage our own emotions, as well as recognise and empathise with the emotions of others and is commonly defined by four attributes.

Self-Awareness

You recognise and perceive your own emotions in the moment and how they affect your thoughts and behaviours. You know your strengths and weaknesses and have self-confidence. Self-awareness includes staying on top of your reactions to events, challenges and people.

We need to maintain healthy levels of self-awareness to be effective. Our ability to express ourselves clearly, to make decisions and to know our own mind all demand self-awareness. Our ability to stay flexible is also related to our self-awareness. Being self-aware can help you recognise strengths, weaknesses and development needs.

Ask yourself: How do people experience you, generally? How might you be described by others? What do you need to stop or start doing to become more self-aware?

Self-Management

This is what happens when you do or do not act. You're able to control impulsive feelings and behaviours, manage your emotions in healthy ways, take initiative, follow through on commitments and adapt to changing circumstances. It's about staying flexible and directing your behaviour positively.

Self-management is the ability to influence ourselves and to choose our responses and behaviour. This relates and applies to both the short and longer term. For example, your ability to make a tough decision and to stick with it, adapt your natural behaviours for the 'greater good' or the longer-term benefit of yourself or others and do something you don't feel like doing.

Self-management builds perfectly on self-awareness because it's one thing to be aware of our natural feelings or tendencies, but it is another to be able to consciously choose what to do in a situation.

Ask yourself: How well do you express and deal with your emotions at work? How well do you handle yourself in difficult situations? What are you doing to enhance your self-management?

Social Awareness

This is your ability to pick up on emotions in other people and to understand what's going on. You have empathy. You can understand the emotions, needs, and concerns of other people, pick up on emotional cues, feel comfortable socially and recognise the power dynamics in a group or organisation. You'll consider the perspectives of other people. The social awareness of others refers to our ability to observe other people and appreciate what is going on with them.

Ask yourself: How good are you at relating to other people? During conversations, how well are you able to interpret the emotional state of the person you are talking to? What are you doing to adapt to meet the other person's needs?

Relationship Management

You know how to develop and maintain good relationships, communicate clearly, inspire and influence others, work well in a team and manage conflict. This taps into the abilities of the three attributes above to manage interactions successfully.

It's skills such as building relationships, harmonising relationships and sustaining relationships over time that affect our ability to communicate clearly with others, to collaborate with others, to negotiate and to deal with conflict successfully, as well as to motivate and manage others well. Interacting and engaging intuitively with others fosters better support within our working relationships and strengthens our opportunity for more open conversations within our relationships and better management of them over time.

Ask yourself: How well do you handle conflict? How effective are you at ethically influencing and negotiating with others? What would we observe in you to know that you are successful in these scenarios?

The Importance of Emotional Intelligence and Psychological Safety

Think back to my 2006 meeting. Everyone in that meeting stayed silent whilst the 'boss' unloaded. No one asked questions. We all sunk straight into 'let's cover our backsides' mode. Some even justified it with blame and finger-pointing.

No one took the time to consider the learnings and how, if we worked together to move things forward, we could have recognised one another's role to play in the outcome and supported each other through it. Instead, there was reaction, heightened emotions, division and a rapidly forming 'us and them' situation instead of a collective and collaborative approach. It was very abrupt, even a tad confrontational, and highly focused on a command and control style directive. It was unquestionably led with fear. The contract would potentially be at risk because of the late deployment. That would mean our jobs could become at risk and the growth of the company held back.

Were we late in the deployment? Yes. Were mistakes made? Yes, without question. But there wasn't a whole lot of ownership being offered up, where things were potentially at great risk. No one in that meeting asked, "What can we do to fix this?" We almost all accepted the status quo because of how that meeting had been led from the top down.

I like to think that people are not defined by the negative behaviours that show up when their backs are pressed to the wall and they are under pressure. In those moments, sometimes we react in an unhelpful way. We might be short and snappy and bark out orders or demands, but it is precisely these moments where we can help a person reset. We can diffuse a situation by demonstrating great emotional intelligence and psychological safety.

I know I've painted a dark picture of the person chairing that meeting that day, but the truth is, overall, they were a great leader and manager. However, at that moment, their frustrations got the better of them and we all felt the repercussions. A few people highlighted this to them afterwards and I know that they were genuinely appalled by their own behaviour.

Some subgroups had ventured off to find solutions and alternatives because we were all invested in ensuring this wouldn't fail. We were all brought back together and apologies were made. Humility and admitting any fallibility is a powerful gift, as is the gift of a genuine apology.

Lesson learned? Absolutely. The next meeting was so much better. The message was still that our project was delayed but this time, there were no outbursts. There was an admittance to a lack of self-awareness and self-management in the previous meeting and this time, it was coupled with inviting the feedback and perspectives of others, understanding the picture we were all facing on our piece of the jigsaw and how this collectively connected with everyone else involved. It was this approach that strengthened us all as a project team that day. We learned from each other, we understood each other, we took time, we were patient, yet we brought about purposeful and intentional action that made good progress. We communicated to the client with honesty and integrity. We presented our challenges and how we were working on a resolution and they were supportive and understanding. Of course, they were keen on a quick resolution and turnaround to get the project live but they commended us on our approach and how we worked well together.

In the end, the project went live with a two-week delay. A lot of lessons were learned and a lot of relationships were strengthened, too.

How Does Your Emotional Intelligence Show Up?

Think about yourself and perhaps some of the questions you answered earlier in the chapter. Developing our emotional intelligence is a way to create the best version of ourselves, or perhaps a better version of ourselves. I like to focus on ways to improve all the time.

I try not to compare myself to others, which is difficult. Instead, I compare myself against myself and focus on becoming a better version of my previous self – whether that's a better me from five years ago, five months ago or five minutes ago. It's a learning journey and I like to ask myself two questions, both very similar and borrowed from the world of Clean Language.

Answer these for yourself now too, out loud, in your head or on your notepad. You can even ask another person for their feedback, too.

Think of these two questions as an emotional intelligence self-audit:

1. *When I am at my best, I'm like... what?*
2. *When I am not at my best, I'm like... what?*

Here's mine:

When I am at my best... I'm like a steam train, happily, steadily and steadfastly progressing down the track, tooting that horn, wooooo wooooooo, having a grand old time.

When I am not at my best... I'm like a grumpy wee pigeon, stoating around, being a little bit edgy.

These two questions can help us identify our emotional intelligence strengths and perhaps some of our current limitations.

For example, I'm a person who needs to pay attention to my self-management, particularly in times of high stress or pressure. I'm a person who says yes to a lot of things, probably too many, but I never say yes to something I don't want to do; I just take on too much at any one time. And this is where my lack of self-management shows up.

If I am overwhelmed, I can become irritable, a tad ratty (or a little bit edgy), you know, short and snappy (usually with a loved one ☹) and maybe feature on the shitty committee for a short spell of time. I'm the first to admit that I can lose patience and have a bit of a 'chop-chop' mentality. It's in these moments that I can also go insular. I'll retreat and become quiet. I'm aware of this, so my self-awareness is high, but I do have to dig deep and really work on my self-management. *How do I do that?* I'll come to that when we come to the Pause Ponder Pounce section.

But, when I am at my best, I feel amazing. I can handle the stresses and pressures and take them in my stride. I am calm and kind, even when faced with difficulties. I look for solutions or alternatives and ways to make changes and/or move forward. I'm balanced.

What does this look like for you?

Doing this quick reflective assessment can bring about a whole host of realisations on our strategies or patterns of behaviour and how they are helping or hindering us.

Helping team members with this can be helpful too. This is where that social awareness aspect of emotional intelligence really comes into its own. Recognising strategies or patterns of behaviour or the representation of feelings and emotions is a powerful gift. Being able to hold space for someone in those moments too is such a privilege – coupled with some supportive conversations, constructive feedback and coaching, it can aid powerful mindset shifts that help us move forward, especially in those moments when a person, either ourselves or another, has become stuck in something like a loop, a rabbit hole or whatever name you want to substitute.

For me, if I don't self-manage, I'll go down a rabbit hole of self-sabotage. My pattern is overwhelm, then procrastination followed by frustration and then the grumpy edgy pigeon appears. **I'm giving myself a micro expression eye roll here *.*

Strengthening Our Own Emotional Intelligence Across Our Businesses

Again, a whole book could be dedicated and written on the topic of emotional intelligence and many do exist on the subject in its entirety. This section discusses the strength of applying emotional intelligence across our businesses. For me, that is in caring and understanding enough about yourself and others and in bringing it to your conscious awareness. It's in being adaptable in any given situation and within the company of others, parallel to managing and regulating our own emotions whilst demonstrating empathy (which also has its own chapter, exciting).

It's about getting our finger on the pulse and knowing what helps to keep that pulse in check. Enter the *PULSE model* – because I like a model, as you now know, and perhaps it might be of use to you and others too, as it's short and sweet and easy to remember.

Perception

This is about being aware, not just of your own emotions, but also those of others. It's like having a sixth sense for feelings, noticing subtle cues, clues and vibes.

Understanding

Think of this as your emotional toolkit. You learn to put words to your feelings, manage them effectively and empathise with others' experiences.

Leadership

Here's where you step up as the emotional guide. You lead by example, resolve conflicts with empathy and foster teamwork and collaboration. Really, role-modelling excellence.

Social

Communication is key here. You express yourself clearly, listen attentively and build strong relationships based on trust and respect.

Empowerment

This is about taking charge of your emotions and helping others do the same. You learn to manage yourself better and support others on their emotional journey.

Engage, Transform, Supercharge 'Emotional Intelligence' Summary

Well, we've covered a chunk of that already but use the below along with the PULSE model and earlier questions to really bring your emotional intelligence to the forefront of your mind.

In summary, in the workplace, emotional intelligence isn't just a buzzword, it's a game-changer and it's in your DNA. It's about understanding ourselves and others on a deeper level and navigating the ups and downs of work relationships. Imagine walking into the office or landing in a Teams call or Zoom meeting and feeling like you're entering a space where you're truly understood and supported. That's the power of emotional intelligence.

Engage

Engagement is key for many things, especially here. It's about tuning into our own emotions and recognising how they affect our interactions, then, extending that understanding to our colleagues, picking up on their cues and making everyone feel valued and included. And let's not forget about relationship management - it's all about building bridges, not walls, and resolving conflicts with empathy.

Transform

Transformation is where leadership really shines. Lead by example (it sounds cliché, but it is absolutely required), show vulnerability and empathy, setting the tone for the whole team. Provide training and development opportunities for the emotional stuff – it's not woolly or fluffy or woo woo, we all have emotions, and we cannot switch them off at the workplace door or Zoom waiting room. Take that mindset and put it right in the bin! Giving everyone a toolkit for navigating emotions in the workplace is about fostering a culture where learning and growth *'is what we do around here'*, and where everyone feels seen and heard.

Supercharge

Supercharging emotional intelligence takes it up a gear and creates an environment where your people can thrive, mentally, emotionally, personally and professionally. It's about integrating emotional intelligence into everything you do and every aspect of what you do, right from recruitment and all the way through to performance reviews. It's about tracking your progress, celebrating our win, and always striving to be the best version of yourself, even the one from just five minutes ago or the one when you happened to lose your shit – and, of course, working on reducing those occasions too, which, ultimately, is a much better way to expend your energy by being emotionally supported and providing that space for others to supercharge theirs too.

Let's Not Stop Here: keep the momentum going and refer to the Emotional Intelligence Toolkit section in your downloadable workbook. Share it with your team and use this as an action plan to work on together.

www.dnacoach.co.uk/leadersassembleworkbook

FROM 'ME' TO 'WE'

3

FROM 'ME' TO 'WE'

Shaping an Empathetic Mindset at Work

Empathy deserves its own chapter. It's such an important thing to have and to display in life, in general, and certainly in the workplace environment.

We all know that workplaces have changed massively in recent years and I alluded to something at the end of the last chapter that never ever sat well with me and is something I have heard repeated in workplaces for years (albeit less so since 2020) and that's the phrase (or instruction as it was dictated to me back in the day) of:

"When you arrive at your work, you leave your home and personal life at the door."

Let's rip that untruth right up and tear it into very tiny and irreparable pieces. How this has ever been a thing, I will never know, as it is just not possible to fulfil. It's a myth at best and bullshit at worst, spouted by mini dictators in the workplace aiming to squeeze every ounce of productivity from people.

Phew, I'm glad I got that off my chest.

I'd like to think this phrase was bandied about because people didn't know how to deal with the outside-of-work stuff and not just that they didn't care. In my early days of working, I had two jobs (well, three, actually) – I worked in bar restaurants, waiting on tables, and in call centres. I also went out singing for my supper of an evening as a local performer, running karaoke and such like.

A bar colleague of mine, who was a friend too, had lost their father and the funeral was a working day of mine at the call centre. The call centre housed 100-plus people.

In my time 'on the phones', I had a number of team managers, some much better than others on the scale of being a good human being. I asked my team manager for a half-day holiday to attend the funeral. This was declined. The reason it was declined is that I hadn't given enough notice and that there weren't enough annual leave hours available, as the percentage of holidays that the centre supported from a workplace planning perspective had been reached. To be really clear here, I had plenty of annual leave to take, the call centre just felt they didn't have enough resources to accommodate it.

But let's circle back to the initial response of "I hadn't given enough notice". Seriously, what on earth? My manager knew my reasons for requesting annual leave. I felt the response took a follow-the-textbook-rules approach that lacked compassion and empathy. It lacked understanding. It was ill-placed. I reacted.

I told my team manager that either way, I would be taking the time off and it wasn't negotiable.

Now, we can debate the nuances of following processes and standards for those who might feel stuck to a rule book all day long, but here's the thing, my friend had lost her father – at nineteen, I might add. I wanted to be there for her, to show my support just like any good friend and human being would want to. I wasn't taking the proverbial. I felt my time was better spent with her than adding on ten-pound top-ups to pay-as-you-go phones for strangers.

I gathered myself following my 'what on earth' reaction and had a conversation with my manager. I actually had to point out what was so wrong with her response and the company procedures in this instance. I had to state that scenarios should be looked at in individual circumstances. I essentially had to ask for empathy to be shown and a human decision to be made.

To cut a long story short, I did get the time off, but it left me feeling like nothing more than a bum on a seat at that point. I didn't feel valued, and I certainly didn't feel understood.

Suffice it to say, we are all SO much more than the person who solely shows up at work. We are not robots, machines, bums on seats or even payroll numbers. We all have stuff going on in our lives that can trickle into our working day.

Even what might seem like 'normal stuff' can weigh on our minds or even just pop into our minds like a walk-on part in a TV show. And here's the cherry on top, most people will now have experienced working from home so the layer of separation between home and work life is even smaller. Those worlds have collided into an entangled mass, big time.

We don't ever really know what goes on behind closed doors, at home or off camera from our Teams calls or Zoom meetings. We may choose to not share our innermost stuff, but that doesn't mean that we can't take a moment to understand what might be going on for another person.

Let's take the example of a person underperforming at work:

Your team member (I hate the expression direct report; it sounds so unhelpfully hierarchical) isn't meeting their targets, objectives or performance measures.

I genuinely want you to think back now and acknowledge how you have approached this conversation with a team member in the past.

Alternatively, if you were the team member not meeting your target, how did someone approach you about that?

I ask these exact questions in the coaching, leadership and psychological safety training programmes I deliver. The responses never cease to astound me. I'll add a caveat here, that many people who do share examples of negative experiences are often sharing examples from their past employers, so there is definitely a shift already evident, which makes me happy.

As before in this book, note down your own experiences and observations. We want the good, the bad and the indifferent and we will come back to them in a short while.

Defining Empathy

There's a way to approach conversations like this with empathy.

Firstly, let's define empathy as this often comes up in conversation, especially around differences between empathetic and empathy and also between empathy and sympathy.

Here are the dictionary definitions:

Empathy (noun)

The ability to imagine and understand the thoughts, perspectives and emotions of another person.

Empathetic (adjective)

Able to understand how somebody else feels because you can imagine what it is like to be that person (also empathic)

- an empathetic listener
- and empathetic to/towards somebody/something

Empathic (adjective)

Involving, characterised by, or based on empathy: EMPATHETIC.

Sympathy (noun)

Feelings of pity and sorrow for someone else's misfortune or (an expression of) understanding and care for someone else's suffering.

Empathic is more often used to describe a person who's an 'empath', a term that means someone who strongly feels other people's feelings. Whereas empathetic is more often used to describe anyone who is able to feel other people's feelings and experiences. Lately, however, the words empathetic and empathic are used interchangeably.

Empathy and sympathy are both related to understanding and sharing the feelings of others, but they involve different levels of emotional involvement and perspective-taking. Sympathy is feeling compassion, sorrow, or pity for the hardships that another person encounters. Empathy is putting yourself in the shoes of another.

Empathy can often be difficult for someone to articulate as a definition, mostly due to the fact that it is something that we feel or think.

For example, have you ever felt nervous on someone else's behalf? Sounds odd, doesn't it, but I bet you have.

Maybe you've:

- Felt butterflies, or that your heart or pulse was racing for someone that you know personally who was about to do something
- Felt a lump in your throat when watching someone tearful on the TV or in a movie
- Felt a rush of excitement or joy when someone shared some good news
- Or finally, experience a surge of pride and happiness as a loved one celebrates an achievement, even if it's not your own accomplishment

These are all examples of empathy.

Empathy can create strong bonds, allowing us to support and relate to others in times of joy or hardship. Professionally, it's central to effective leadership, teamwork, and relationship building.

Empathetic people in the workplace, whether they are leaders or colleagues, can motivate and inspire others and better understand their clients or customer needs. All of these things lead to better approaches, better workplaces and better cultures and point towards us being part of a better place to work.

How we experience or display empathy will vary from person to person. We all experience the world differently and this experience is subjective based on how we think, our values, our beliefs and our own perceptions. Think of this example, you go to the cinema with a pal or a partner and watch the same movie yet one of you laughs or cries at parts that the other doesn't. We can all look at the same thing, and yet see, think or feel something different. Everyone has their own worldview/model.

But what we can all do is to practise it and to demonstrate it within the workplace. By doing so we promote kindness, cooperation, collaboration and overall well-being, both personally and professionally.

Empathy in the workplace means having the ability to understand the needs of others and being aware of their feelings and thoughts. However, it has often been overlooked as a performance indicator and merely as a 'soft skill' (I hate the negative connotations around this phrase. I will come back to that later).

In fact, empathy is a **power skill** that can be developed (even for those who say they are not a naturally empathetic person) because it's about creating a person-focused or person-centred culture. It's about being able to work well with people from varying teams, departments, countries, cultures and backgrounds. And it is in demonstrating empathy in the workplace that we discover that emotional intelligence is a key part of both personal and professional effectiveness.

Empathy is a fundamental quality that contributes to a positive and productive workplace culture. It promotes a sense of belonging among team members, increasing psychological safety, staff satisfaction and engagement, productivity and success. And if that's not what you want in your organisation or from your role, then you absolutely need to read this entire book, even more so than perhaps you first thought.

Demonstrating an Empathetic Approach and Mindset

I said I would come back to it and now I am: what did you have noted down from earlier? I often hear feedback from people that leaders and managers can come across as too task or results-focused or have an all-business attitude and lack a people approach.

When this is the sole approach, it can negatively fuel the mindset of team members that they are merely a payroll number or a bum on the seat. They feel and see no value in themselves and the organisation. Team members won't then speak up or ask for help or come to you with ideas, questions and suggestions, which all link back to why we should be embedding a clear culture of psychological safety within our workplaces and teams.

When we demonstrate an empathetic approach and mindset, not just for the problems a person may face or the underperformance I mentioned earlier, it opens up our human approach – the approach that everyday leadership style revolves around being person-centred. An empathetic approach aids in comprehending the motivations and emotional states of our team members. This can help us to understand and solve any discontent or stress or assist with personal issues and even any conflict issues.

It can also help us to recognise any behavioural changes or signs of distress in our colleagues that could be impacting their well-being, productivity, focus or mindset.

To demonstrate empathy is to take a moment to pause and consider what might be going on for the person in front of us, inside and outside of work, internally and externally in their thoughts or their behaviour.

If we lead with empathy by listening, offering our support, asking what we can do and providing our support or any resource, we show that we understand and we validate what that person is experiencing and feeling in the moment, even if we don't agree.

Ask yourself these questions:

- In what ways do you currently incorporate empathy into your interactions with colleagues or team members?
- How do you think cultivating empathy among team members could positively impact collaboration and productivity?
- What will you do to recognise what's going on for your colleagues?
- When you do notice what's going on for them (or it is brought to your attention), how will you deal with the person and the things they are experiencing in an empathetic way?

This chapter neatly dovetails with the next few chapters around feedback, my model of Pause-Ponder-Pounce and having everyday coaching conversations too, but for now, here's a summary of how we Engage, Transform and Supercharge by having an empathetic mindset and approach.

Engage, Transform, Supercharge 'Empathy' Summary

Engage

As leaders, we need to engage with empathy right from the start. Again, it's in your DNA and it's about more than just hearing our team members – it's about truly listening, understanding and validating their experiences. By fostering an environment where everyone feels safe to express themselves, we build trust and strengthen our connections with our team. We need to listen deeply to what team members say, and also listen for what they don't say – sometimes we need to tease that out. Listen, don't judge or assume, and then enquire by the use of some great questions.

Transform

Empathy isn't another buzzword and it's not a fluffy or wishy-washy response – it's a way of being. It starts with us leading by example with authenticity and openness. We can transform our approach to empathy from a mere concept or ideal into a true living and breathing example and reality. If we integrate empathy into our decision-making and daily interactions, we create a culture of understanding and compassion where it then becomes 'what we do around here', considering at all stages what we are doing and saying and how that would be viewed and understood by another person.

Supercharge

To supercharge and take the empathetic approach to the next level, we need to embed it deeply into the DNA of our organisation, at every single level. It's about weaving empathy into everything, our values, our policies, our procedures, our everyday practices and our interactions. Ultimately, by putting empathy at the core of everything we do at every level, we create a workplace culture where empathy isn't just encouraged – it's celebrated.

Let's Not Stop Here: keep the momentum going and refer to the Empathetic Mindset Toolkit section in your downloadable workbook. Share it with your team and use this as an action plan to work on together.

www.dnacoach.co.uk/leadersassembleworkbook

FEEDBACK IS A GIFT...

4

FEEDBACK IS A GIFT…

But be careful there’s not a shit present inside!

I remember hearing the phrase ‘feedback is a gift’ years ago. I can’t quite recall where it was said or who said it and at first, I liked the phrase, and part of me still does, but then I observed and heard really shitty feedback being given under this guise of ‘a gift’ and I decided to add to the phrase.

Are you ready for it? Well, the clue is in the chapter subtitle above, so it’s probably not a surprise, but say it out loud with me anyway.

Feedback is a gift… but be careful there’s not a shit present inside.

I’ve even bought gift wrapping paper that says, `’shit present inside`’. I wrap little feedback statements in it and use it as a prop for a training session on the art of feedback for leaders and managers. Because giving feedback is an art (and that's not meant to sound cheesy or cliched). It involves skill and it can be a gift as long as the 'gift giver' shares feedback in a way that is helpful.

Note the word 'share' here because feedback should be a sharing opportunity. Feedback isn't one-dimensional or one-directional. There is feedback in absolutely everything. It's everywhere and it's all around us and we should be willing to share feedback by giving it and receiving it, noticing it and hearing it and, ultimately, using it as an opportunity to do something.

Feedback is a communication method and we actually learn it at a very young age as a learning process, but we probably didn't consider it to be feedback. Think about touching something hot as a child. If we touch that hot thing, we experience pain receptors, and our brain processes that information knowing not to touch it again. Well, that is feedback.

You'll have observed feedback before when watching a person's expressions, perhaps their facial reactions or gestures. Feedback.

You'll have read reviews of something, maybe a movie or a travel destination. Feedback.

Maybe you've submitted something like a report or an assignment for review or assessment and received your grade with some commentary. Feedback.

It is literally everywhere, and I am sure you can think of many more examples besides the ones I've shared.

There are many publications and articles on how to share feedback and a ton of models to use when sharing feedback. Doing a quick Google search for feedback models will give you many responses with some great resources, but I'd like to peddle it backwards first, with some background to feedback, before sharing a model/practice with you.

In my first proper job, the one I told you about at the beginning of the book, I worked in a contact centre and I was very good at my job as a customer service advisor. As a part of my role, I would have regular, one-to-one, performance reviews with my team manager. You'd be presented with your quality results in these meetings, and on one occasion my results were only 95% and not the usual 100% I had become accustomed to. I was horrified. My line manager Stewart shared with me the feedback, very factually and with kindness but my shutter was down and my padlock was on. I went into defence mode. Essentially, I had missed a very small step which didn't have a customer impact but dropped me down a few percentage points. I burst out crying. Poor Stewart is all I can say. I descended into a short-term state of rigour-mortis rigidity whilst the tears streamed, snot ran from my nose and I was wailing. Stewart emerged from his state of brief paralysis and shared with me that this very small score drop didn't define me as a person and that the feedback he shared was helpful for me to recognise that occasionally, we get things wrong and that can be a useful space to learn from but that I had to be willing to listen. I could go down a very long list of other conversational points from that feedback session but the thing that sticks out is that Stewart had shared with me that feedback is a learning experience, even for the good stuff. It's not a reflection of who we are. I was still very good at my job, just not 100% perfect on that occasion and that was ok.

I reflected on that one-to-one review with Stewart a lot over the years that followed and learned to be open and receptive to feedback - good, bad and indifferent - as there will be something to learn in it, perhaps even something actionable to change or to move forward with.

Now, back to the concept of feedback being a gift yet beware of the shit present inside.

The Shit Gift

Over the years, I've gone on to hear lots more feedback, either directly said to me or that I've observed or witnessed others giving, and cringed.

Some feedback statements lead with:

You did well on this, but...
This worked well, but...
Here's what you should do...
You need to do better...
You're not quite getting it...

These are *ALL* the types of statements that keep people in a stuck state, and they become judgemental and opinion-based. I refer to these as 'Judgy Judgerson' statements.

We also have people hiding behind the guise of being candid but actually coming across as a tad mean. We can be explicit in what we want to express without being meanies and hiding behind the ruse of candour (or candor for our American English fans).

Feedback should be regular, helpful, constructive, conducive, growth-inspired, future-driven, supportive and factual. It should not be opinionated, judgemental or vague, and it should all be action-focused.

I am going to address the word constructive here as I hear it way too many times, accompanied by the word criticism.

Here's a mic drop moment. Constructive criticism is not a thing. We could debate the linguistic nuances of this all day long but hear me out.

Constructive yes, criticism no.

Of course, the intent behind the phrase constructive criticism is to represent an approach to providing feedback that seeks to build and improve rather than tear down or discourage.

Using the word criticism can feel a bit harsh. This doesn't mean there is a need for us to turn into a 'fluffy wuffy', blowing smoke type of person but there is definitely a way to share feedback that doesn't have the most brutal of criticism attached to it.

Instead, consider it as, 'constructive feedback', helpful feedback, or, as I like to refer to it, *Future Focused Feedback* (I also am a fan of an alliteration).

Future Focused Feedback

We can share feedback with a few things in mind - psychological safety, empathy and a growth mindset. These three things are what future-focused feedback is all about.

It's quite common to hear that feedback is mainly shared when something doesn't quite go to plan. Maybe a mistake is made, or a target or goal is not reached, for example. Feedback can be very useful as a reflective practice to learn from.

However, feedback should be an everyday practice and not something that is solely shared when things go wrong. Feedback is hugely beneficial in the context of recognition, too. Feedback isn't something to be feared and only shared when something negative is being said.

Feedback *is* a gift.

I studied NLP (Neuro Linguistic Programming) many years ago and one of the principles or presuppositions of NLP is that:

"There is no failure, only feedback."

What I love about this particular statement is the opportunity it presents to consider feedback from a shifted perspective. This is because it comes from a place of learning and growth and helps us to then shape what our future selves can be, have, do and change, along with what we can achieve.

Feedback is a growth mindset opportunity where we can think about the power of having no failure and accept that there is only feedback.

Let's take an example from life like learning to drive or taking a test or an exam.

Who here (speaking out loud from my page right now) has ever passed something but not on the first attempt? Go on, raise your hand or give a nod if this is you.

Ok, so, full disclosure, I did pass my practical driving test on my first attempt yet, I know many who passed on attempt two, three or even four.

I failed my maths test three times in school before passing, yet some friends passed on their first or second attempt.

I failed my Scottish Standard Grade science exam (GCSE equivalent back in the day), yet went on to pass my Standard Grade biology exam instead. I did this because I failed at one but decided to niche down and go for the other. I found the chemistry element of Standard Grade science and a little bit of physics beyond me, but I loved biology so decided I'd pass that instead, and I did.

I want you to notice my intentional use of the word, yet.

You may not have passed your driving test or exam on the first attempt but in some respects, you will have reframed your thinking and mindset to the power of 'yet' if you retake the driving test or exam. You may not have said it out loud, but the mindset will have been there to consider that you just haven't passed... yet. Because you took it again. Maybe you reflected on the things that meant you didn't pass the first time around and worked to improve upon them. And then you put yourself forward again, you made progress all based on...drum roll please.... feedback and a good dose of yet.

In Carol Dweck's 2006 book, *Mindset*, I had many, "oh, my gosh, that's me," moments to the point where I felt she could have written the book for me personally, (to the point where I had to check her book's dedication page in case I was mentioned). I resonated (and still do) with every word and meaning attached.

She talks about growth mindset environments being ones that:

- Value hard work, determination and perseverance over talent
- Help employees learn new skills through coaching and feedback
- Encourage experimentation and the trying out of new ideas
- Use failures as valuable learning opportunities

- Empower individuals to take responsibility and to own up to their mistakes
- Encourage people to speak up and respect diverse viewpoints
- Give feedback to promote learning and the desire to achieve better.

I adore all of this. This is feedback at its best. This is feedback as a gift, with a delightfully useful present inside.

Dweck talks about a growth mindset as being:
A belief that you're not limited by inherent traits or abilities but rather, have the capacity to learn and grow.

People can be coached or trained to improve their skills, and feedback can play a huge part in this.

Dweck also goes on to highlight those with a fixed mindset as being individuals who:
Believe you possess a certain set of characteristics, like talent or intelligence, that is unlikely to change.

Therefore, the presumption is that those who don't perform well can't ever do better. And it's that presumption that should find its way into the bin.

Feedback that is solely negatively focused or self-limiting helps to fuel the unhelpful thinking pattern of 'I'm not good enough' or 'I have failed' and keeps a person stuck.

It's this that I feel is the mindset that was wrongfully championed in my school days (and likely yours too) and acts as a reminder for me being told by my careers advisor that I wasn't 'clever enough'.

With all of this in mind, it is safe to say that we can change the structure of how we share feedback in the workplace. Feedback should be future-focused and seen as a conversation. It's most definitely not and shouldn't be seen as a one-directional flow. And this is where the sweet spot lies.

Let's take a look at some examples where we may find ourselves entering into a feedback conversation. Now, I have deliberately chosen the awkward subjects that we might have to have a conversation about as typically, these will be the ones that we will want to pay more attention to and get right. And by getting it right, I mean that the feedback shared leaves a person with a learning opportunity that they can take action towards.

All too often, I hear people fearing feedback because it's typically something they hear when underperformance occurs. I want to tip that balance and ask you to consider how feedback is provided by you and overall, throughout your organisation.

So here are the less-than-fun scenarios to consider:

- Dealing with the late delivery of a piece of work such as a project or report submission
- Dealing with the unprofessional and non-psychologically safe behaviour of a team member that goes against company values

- Dealing with underperformance where a team member has not met their targets.

It would be very easy in these scenarios to form opinions and judgements on why these are the outcomes. For example, we could judge a person who has missed a deadline as not being organised enough or disciplined enough or for having a non-committal attitude towards a deadline. Or, we could make assumptions that a person who has had an outburst or has been short and snappy is generally just an asshat. Or, we could feel that when a person hasn't reached their targets they are just not cutting it and this isn't the job for them.

It would again be very easy to jump to these conclusions, but they are certainly not helpful ways to think about a colleague or team member. These are potentially 'mean mind reads' into a scenario that is formed because we perhaps have a bias towards a person, or we are still living in the world of command-and-control styles of leadership.

Task: spend a few minutes considering the following (grab your pad and note your responses)...

As a phenomenal leader or manager, if these 'less-than-fun' scenarios were to occur with your team member, how would you approach the conversation? What would you need to find out first? What style of approach would you take? What questions would you ask them? How would you help your team member to make a considered change and to create steps to move forward?

A useful way to engage in feedback is conversationally and ideally, rather than you as the leader or manager sharing your feedback first, ask your team members to reflect and share their observations before you share yours.

As the phenomenal leader or manager that you are, I want you to tap into the responses you noted down a moment ago about approaching the conversation with empathy and a supportive style. We never know what's going on for another person. People tend not to show up at work wanting to get things wrong or to not meet their objectives. Most people, if not all, want to do their very best and if something isn't quite supporting that, then meeting our colleagues first and foremost at a level of support is always the approach to lead with.

Ask questions to help your team members identify any root causes for whatever they are experiencing or demonstrating right now. Find out from them what they need help with or what they are struggling with and anything that's getting in the way for them.

Genuinely enquire how they are. Check in that they are okay. Even more so if the less-than-fun scenarios are out of character or not the norm for your colleague.

The Three-Staged Framework

A practice I actively encourage leaders and managers to adopt when having a future-focused feedback conversation is to use our *Three-Staged Framework approach*. The Opener, The Observation and The Opportunity.

Keeping all of the above in mind, let's use the less-than-fun topic of underperformance, with a team member not making their target this month, as our framework example.

Stage One - The Opener

This is where you open up the conversation to engage and encourage your team member to share their feedback first and where you truly listen to their responses. You might use openers such as:

- How have things been going? How are you getting on?
- How has the month gone for you?
- What's worked well and/or not so well for you?

Stage Two - The Observation

This is the part where you share any of your observations or reflections on what your team member has shared and ask some more questions on ideas, they might have that can help them make change and to move forward. This is aimed at leading them towards transformation.

Note that when sharing observations, it's best to start with a lead in line of "I noticed that..."

For example, "I noticed that you were on target up until...", then ask:

- What might you need help with?
- What resources or ideas do you have?
- What would be useful for you right now?
- On reflection, what have you observed or noticed?
- What habits or practices are helping or hindering you?

Stage Three - The Opportunity

This is the part where you help your team members to supercharge through supported actions.

- What could or will you do?
- What would you like to change or do differently?
- What will you continue with that's working well?
- What do you need or want from me?
- How will you approach this going forward?
- What's your first step?
- When shall we review your progress?

When carrying out any feedback conversation and when using our framework, remember that we are so much more than the person who shows up for work. We cannot possibly switch off our minds fully and we can sometimes get distracted or waylaid by things outside of work. How many of us can relate to any of these situations:

- Care requirements for a family member
- Moving house
- Household emergencies
- Sickness
- Bereavements
- Personal appointments
- Relationship issues

I remember moving house and the constant back and forth, dealing with estate agents and solicitors was overwhelming. People say that a house move is one of the most stressful things you will ever do, and it's true. For me, the moving part is a breeze compared to the arranging of the legal and financial stuff beforehand. And of course, these businesses are typically open Monday to Friday, nine to five, when we, too, are at work. So, it's only natural that these pressures and situations will creep into our workspaces, even when we do our best for them not to.

As leaders and managers, we should have a vested interest in ensuring our people are set up for success, so checking in with ourselves can be useful. Ask yourself these questions:

- Has my team member had appropriate training to enable them to be successful in this task, piece of work or situation?
- Were there clearly defined and agreed parameters, timeframes and objectives that everyone understood?

- Were there enough check-ins with my team member to review their progress and have I asked how they are getting on?
- Did we check that the team member has the capacity to take on this piece of work?

If the answer to any of these is no, then this is the opportunity to support, shape and influence the environment around you and your colleagues for success.

Stop, Start, Continue

Of all the feedback models out there in the big bad world, I also quite like the simple and straightforward Stop, Start, Continue model, often attributed to the Gallup Organisation as its creator. I use this for myself as a self-feedback and coaching model as well as with others personally and professionally.

In its simplest form, it's a great tool where we reflect on what we want to or need to start doing (or begin), what we want to or need to stop doing (or avoid) and what we want to or need to continue (or maintain) doing.

I used it to manage my time when writing this book so that I didn't fall into the less-than-fun scenario of missing a deadline (I'm easily distracted). I stopped procrastinating, I started time blocking and I continued prioritising writing over less immediate activities.

But what if we did fail (or perceived that we had)?

On a personal (and professional) level, if you ever do feel that there has been a failure, or a perception of failure, rather than success, try using these self-coaching questions to help:

- What happened? Or didn't happen?
- On a scale of one-ten (ten being catastrophic), how bad is the situation, really?
- How important will it be in three or six months? In twelve months? In three years?
- Are you reacting or responding?
- What can you do to improve the situation?
- How will you make the best/most appropriate response?
- What learning can you take from this?
- What positives can you take from this?
- What will you do now?
- What will you do differently?

I encourage everyone to look objectively at what can be resolved here and what can we do now. We can, of course, learn from the past, but we can never change it.

Our overall approach in having future-focused feedback conversations is that throughout the conversation, we demonstrate empathy and understanding towards the colleague's perspective. Encourage collaboration and open dialogue to empower the team members to problem-solve and make decisions.

Feedback should always be action-oriented. Focus on identifying actionable steps and setting clear goals for improvement, following up and tracking progress, providing ongoing support and not being afraid to adjust actions as needed/or required.

Before we head to recognition and the wonderful world of coaching, let's do a final short and sweet summary of how we can Engage, Transform and Supercharge through future-focused feedback.

Engage, Transform, Supercharge 'Feedback' Summary

Engage

It's about fostering a workplace culture where feedback is not just about pointing out past mistakes but about envisioning future possibilities.

Transform

Our role in transforming our feedback approach is key. We want to enable team members to look ahead and proactively support them in achieving their future goals.

Supercharge

Remember, there is feedback in everything. Reframe any negative connotation of feedback to let it be seen as a catalyst for growth and progress.

Let's Not Stop Here: keep the momentum going and refer to the Future Focused Feedback Toolkit section in your downloadable workbook. Share it with your team and use this as an action plan to work on together.

www.dnacoach.co.uk/leadersassembleworkbook

RECOGNITION IGNITION

5
RECOGNITION IGNITION

Nurturing Acknowledgement and Appreciation

In creating a great place to work, it's important to recognise your team members. This can be done in a number of ways such as highlighting effort, progress, contribution, successes and achievements. This helps to create a workplace culture of recognition which directly links to having a culture that is psychologically safe.

Think how lovely it feels when someone acknowledges what you are doing or have already done, when you get thanks for it, when they celebrate you within it and when they share the accolades with you – it's empowering, inspiring and motivational. In those moments, we feel appreciated, valued and seen. We feel validated that someone has taken notice of the work we are doing and the part that we play. We feel rewarded and regarded. It can help boost engagement and, of course, directly links to continued improved performance, enhancing quality outputs, better staff retention and higher levels of employee satisfaction as well as overall well-being.

When we don't pay any recognition towards the efforts of others, the opposite occurs. Team members feel exploited, they feel like 'just a number' and possibly even get to the stage of feeling so unmotivated that they lack any desire to stay in that role or even with that same organisation.

Companies can often assume that to recognise staff members there has to be a financial incentive or reward and whilst that is a lovely thing to have, it's not the only thing that we human beings want in our workplace settings.

> When we are recognised, we feel respected. And when we feel respected, we feel included.

Recognising Your Team Members

This can be very simple and straightforward in the everyday human interactions that we have.

Feedback is a great way to recognise your team members. Share what they are working on and the benefits of that along with the values that they are delivering. Don't solely rely on this at quarterly review time or annual appraisals. It can be incorporated into monthly one-to-ones or even weekly check-ins, team meetings, individual catch-ups and companywide gatherings... the list is endless.

Everyday recognition can play a huge part too. I love, love, love the everyday small tokens of appreciation that people share when I ask what things people do in the workplace to recognise colleagues. Thanking co-workers for the effort that day, making a cuppa, sharing treats, celebrating birthdays and organisational milestones (i.e., a year in service) and sharing the small and the larger successes and progress along the way – all of these are great morale boosters and help each person feel a sense of worth and pride in what they do.

Out loud verbal recognition is a biggie for me. Even a simple 'thank you' is an expression that can make a huge difference.

Also, the natural things that we do without realising, like recognising a colleague has a looming deadline and offering our help and support.

Again, this all links back to that role modelling behaviour and the knowledge that our colleagues have our backs. Recognition doesn't have to be one-directional either. For example, it doesn't have to always be the leader or manager recognising the team member. We can do this for our peers, our colleagues, and the leaders and managers above us too.

Take a moment here to think: in what ways could you recognise your fellow colleagues? How would you go about doing this? Take some time to think about this as well as consider how you would like to be recognised by others.

Here are some useful *coaching questions* that can help you along the way and don't forget to ask people to share their own observations. Remember, the first rule of feedback is that we invite our team members to share their reflections first, so, why not ask them to share a recent success story or achievement they've had at work:

- What specific accomplishments have you observed in others?
- What challenges have colleagues overcome to reach their goals?
- What strengths or skills do you feel your team members bring to the team?
- How have they utilised their strengths to contribute to projects or initiatives?
- What unique talents or abilities have you noticed in your colleagues?
- How have team members collaborated with others to achieve shared objectives?
- Has there been a time when they provided support or assistance to a fellow colleague?
- What role do they play in fostering a positive and inclusive team environment?
- How have they implemented innovative ideas or solutions that have positively impacted their own work or the work of others?
- How do they encourage creativity and innovation within your team or department?

Let's link this to how we **Engage**, **Transform** and **Supercharge** to create a great culture of recognition in the workplace.

Engage, Transform, Supercharge 'Recognition' Summary

Engage

Creating a culture of recognition starts with engaging everyone, at all levels in the workplace, on the importance of acknowledgement and appreciation. Ask colleagues how they'd like to be recognised. This can make the experience a lot more personalised if it's genuinely tailored to the individual. It makes it more meaningful. Sharing ideas and suggestions on how to demonstrate gratitude towards one another in the team is also a good way to do this.

Transform

Let's move away from traditional approaches that only acknowledge the 'big successes' at annual appraisal time or end-of-year events. Transform the culture with the recognition that continues to inspire and motivate your people. Share stories at team meetings of learnings, progress, small wins or successes and even learnings from along the way that will help to transform what happens next time. You can even be spontaneous in the way you recognise a team member, maybe a shout-out on your internal comms systems or within your team meetings, perhaps even a small email or message to say thank you.

Supercharge

This is where we can get into the techie stuff. What platforms can you tap into that encourage company-wide, instant recognition at a peer-to-peer level? Provide ongoing updates on the impact of recognition initiatives, share successes and testimonials from employees (and customers or clients) and actively solicit feedback from team members.

Let's Not Stop Here: keep the momentum going and refer to the Recognition Ignition Toolkit section in your downloadable workbook. Share it with your team and use this as an action plan to work on together.

www.dnacoach.co.uk/leadersassembleworkbook

PAUSE
PONDER
POUNCE

6
PAUSE PONDER POUNCE

A Strategy for Intentional Action

This chapter is a little different. I'm going to begin by sharing with you a model that I created during the first COVID-19 lockdown to complement a masterclass webinar on having a resilient mindset I'd produced for the CIPD North East branch members. It was the catalyst for creating my coaching card deck series with the first deck being, **The Resilient Mindset Coaching Card Deck**. You can find info on the card decks at the back of this book.

Of course, the world came to a forced pause during the Coronavirus outbreak and being resilient in our approach was crucial. It made me realise that generally in life, we don't take enough time to pause or to stop and think before we take action. We are living in a world with everything at our fingertips and with instant access to a wealth of information and resources just a few taps away.

Personally, I think this has caused us to have less patience in life, as there always seems to be a sense of urgency because everything is so accessible, or at least much more accessible than it ever was and with much faster timeframes attached.

We've become a world where we don't need to wait. And this shows up in many avenues of life. For example, do you have an Amazon Prime account, and do you prefer to buy items that are Prime eligible because of the next-day delivery? Do you choose a delivery provider or an item that comes with a quicker turnaround rather than wait longer for an alternative?

I practised some patience recently, which is unusual for me as by my very nature, I can be quite an impulsive person, especially around purchases. I decided to buy a new sofa. I wanted the new sofa quickly because I was firm in my decision that the old one had to go. So, I started looking at sofa options that came with a quick delivery turnaround. I saw plenty of lovely sofas, visited the online stores in detail and then went to the showroom to try them out BUT I couldn't get comfortable. I couldn't get comfortable because I was merely selecting at this stage based on the speed of delivery rather than what would be nice to sit and relax on. It was at this point that I decided to pause and think about it in more detail before making my buying decision... which led to purchasing the perfect sofa and exercising patience to wait thirteen weeks for its arrival.

This is a random but relatable example of being able to Pause, and then Ponder before Pouncing into action. This may well be the thing that helps you make better decisions, leading to better outcomes both in and outside of the workplace environment.

Let's take a look at the model.

The DNA Coach Three P's Model

I refer to this more often as the *DNA Coach Three P's Model of Pause, Ponder, Pounce*. It's a useful practice or approach (or mindset, even) to use in times when we have competing priorities and varying viewpoints and emotions rattling around in the mix.

The first step, **Pause**, encourages us to take a moment to collect and gather our thoughts, emotions and intentions. It's about slowing down and allowing ourselves the space to consider the situation carefully.

Next comes, **Ponder**. This stage invites us to reflect deeply on what we've gathered during our pause. It's an opportunity to weigh up those various viewpoints, consider potential consequences, recognise and manage those emotions and refine our message or what comes next to ensure it aligns with our intentions.

Finally, we **Pounce**, *with precision*. Ready with a well-considered response, we confidently and thoughtfully communicate, navigating through competing priorities, differing perspectives and complex emotions to achieve positive actions and outcomes. This is where we take action in a congruent and ethical way, aligned with our values.

Consider the scenario...

You are having a howler of a day. You miss the bus to work, and you arrive feeling flustered. You're feeling a tad Edgy Edgerson (Judgy Judgerson's cousin). Someone sends you an email following up on something that you have yet to provide. This email starts, "As per my last email..."

How do you respond?

I'm chuckling even as I'm typing this. My brain was instantly shifting into a fight response. Yours probably is, too. I was ready to react. How many of us have done this? Reacted in a moment and lost our shit? It's unhelpful for all parties involved, isn't it?

And that's the message. It is all about being able to choose our response, taking a pause, so we can ponder and then pounce with precision, rather than reacting in the moment.

The Three P's model can help with this. It's a pattern interrupter. It's the response that engages our minds just before we roll those sleeves up to hammer out an unhelpful response.

It starts with a breath.

That breath is a deep inhale, filling our lungs and pushing it right into our bellies (diaphragm technically, but I like the word belly).

That deep breath shifts us into a calmer state (to *Pause*), where our rational response lives.

And you stay there with it, even if it's just for a couple of seconds – longer if you need to.

You might even tap into your flight mode just for a moment. I encourage you to get up, step away from the email reply button and grab a cuppa or step outside and breathe in the blue of the sky.

This gives us time because we're paused.

We can now *Ponder*. Think about how we wish to respond. What will be the best course of action here? Maybe even consider how the other person is feeling at the other end of the 'as per my last email' message. You might not spend a lot of time here, it may even be just a minute or two, but that can be enough to give you a choice in what you do next.

You return to your desk and you respond. How is that response different now from the initial reaction you had? This is where you're able to *Pounce* into helpful action. And this is where you don't *pounce* unhelpfully at that person.

We can use this adaptable model in so many ways and so many scenarios – as a strategy for completing a task or piece of work, or an action point you took at a meeting, or even when tensions are high, and you want to avoid something turning into an unhelpful conflict.

It's a great and impactful model that's easy to share with your team too. It links back to being self-aware and demonstrates emotional intelligence, empathy and psychological safety, too.

Here's a little more on each of the Three P's model.

Pause

Pausing allows you to bring your whole self into your work and life. It helps you to spend time on the things that matter most. Taking the time to pause will benefit your resilience and your productivity.

A well-intentioned pause allows you to consciously respond to situations rather than to react out of habit. Pausing replenishes our reserves by giving the mind and body a rest, a chance to recharge and a chance to move forward in a more considered way. It can also help you to evaluate priorities and adjust your focus along with your goals.

Pausing allows a steady pace, slows down any ill-placed negative reactions and provides a clear route to clarity. A literal 'Pause' in the flow of your breath is a really useful tool to clear the mind and body whilst providing much-needed cognitive space.

Ask yourself these questions:

- Take a moment and consider the different perspectives involved in the current situation.
- What is the most important outcome you hope to achieve in this context?
- How might your initial reaction be perceived by others and does it align with your intended message?
- How can you ensure that your response respects the feelings and perspectives of others involved?

Ponder

Pondering allows you to use thinking time to generate ideas, opportunities and solutions. It's a period to counter difficulties by building the strength and resilience needed to confront setbacks and adversity. Use this time to create and innovate, to find fresh perspectives, to engage positively and to connect or collaborate with others.

Ask yourself these questions:

- What are the options?
- How flexible do you need to be?
- What if you had a setback or an option that did not work?
- How do you think others involved in this situation might perceive your response and what impact could it have on them?

- Are there any potential risks or challenges associated with your initial thoughts or reactions that you need to address during this Ponder phase?

Pounce

Pouncing is about setting things into motion and action. What will you do, what can you do and when? Being able to act following an opportunity to Pause and Ponder allows decisions to be made with clarity and a fair assessment of risk. This will allow you to get on with what is needed in a resilient, calm and clear way.

Ask yourself these questions:

- How can you articulate your response in a way that is clear, concise and aligned with your intentions?
- How will you approach this? What actions will you take and when?
- What support do you need and from whom?
- What specific actions can you take right now to communicate effectively in this situation?
- When will you review your progress?

Engage, Transform and Supercharge 'Three P's' Summary

In following the Three P's model, we can **engage** ourselves to be more ready with helpful responses that will ultimately **transform** how we communicate with ourselves and others. This, in turn, can strengthen and **supercharge** our resolve, our resilience and our relationships.

Let's Not Stop Here: keep the momentum going and refer to the DNA Coach Three P's Toolkit section in your downloadable workbook. Share it with your team and use this as an action plan to work on together.

www.dnacoach.co.uk/leadersassembleworkbook

DEVELOPING A RESILIENT MINDSET

7

DEVELOPING A RESILIENT MINDSET

How to Top Up Our Resilience Reserves

Almost a twinned chapter with the last, this section discusses the world of resilience and how to have a resilient mindset.

As per my last chapter (I couldn't resist throwing in an 'as per'), I delivered some webinars on the subject of resilience during the first lockdown. I went down a research rabbit hole to identify all the different elements that aid people in being resilient, what resilience is and how it then shows up for them in our everyday lives.

I talk with people all the time about being the best version of themselves and being the superhero in their own life stories. I want us all to be the best in everything we do, with many superpowers at our disposal, so that they become ordinary and everyday practices/ behaviours, both personally and professionally.

Growing up, I watched endless superhero-based programmes and movies with Big Stevie (my dad) and I always wanted to have a superpower myself. We would watch the old-school Superman TV series from the 1950s starring George Reeves, Wonder Woman with Linda Carter and a whole lot more. I think this is where my love for Marvel and DC comics and movies comes from, even today.

I'm also a person who looks for metaphors and parallels in life, so I started to consider from quite a young age that the things we as human beings do in this world are quite remarkable. We have many attributes, qualities and gifts that are pretty awesome, especially when they become our everyday, extraordinary superpowers, supporting us through life's trials and tribulations.

This is what resilience can bring.

> Resilience is within us all. It's our ordinary, everyday superpower for the small stuff and the life-changing events that are universal and inevitable.

What is Resilience, Really?

Resilience refers to both the process and outcome of successfully adapting to difficult or challenging life experiences, according to the definition from the American Psychological Association (APA). It's having the mental, emotional and behavioural flexibility and the ability to adjust to both internal and external demands. Resilience is the ability to cope with and recover from setbacks, and it is the ability to not only recover quickly from a crisis but to bounce back better— and even to thrive.

Resilience is not about how much suffering you can take or the pain you can endure. Resilience is not about how much work you can be overloaded with. It's not about pushing or powering through or soldiering on and it's not like a trampoline, where you are up one minute and down the next.

Resilience is your everyday, ordinary superpower, supporting you from the shadows. Resilience allows you to maintain balance under pressure. You already have it within you, but the good news is that you can further develop your skills in it. Resilience can be many things – it's your 'bouncebackability', your capacity to cope, your response to adversity, your ability to recharge and your ability to recover.

Resilience involves successfully adapting to difficult or challenging life experiences, which includes the ability to adjust to both internal and external demands. Here are examples of resilience demands in both personal and professional contexts:

Internal Demands

- Emotional demands coping with intense emotions such as grief, anxiety or depression resulting from personal life events.
- Facing the internal demands that we place upon ourselves that are related to self-esteem and self-confidence when trying to adapt to changes. Overcoming self-doubt requires emotional resilience.
- Managing intrusive thoughts or negative thought patterns that can hinder how we adapt and that may contribute to our anxiety or stress during challenging situations.
- Managing the stress and pressure associated with deadlines, high workloads and job responsibilities is an internal demand. Resilience helps cope with this while maintaining performance and well-being but note, this can also become an external demand if unrealistic and unhealthy pressures are being placed upon us by others in the workplace too.

External Demands

- External demands related to financial stresses, such as mounting debts or unexpected expenses, may require resilience to find solutions and regain financial stability.
- Economic recessions or industry-specific challenges can impact job security and require

resilience to adapt to changes.

- Changes in the workplace such as redundancies, mergers and changes to leadership structures can place external demands on us.
- Advances and changes in technology can add layers of pressure and demand.
- Remote and hybrid working continues to be an added pressure while juggling/balancing the blend that becomes home and work life in one physical location.

Being resilient means effectively coping with these demands and ultimately thriving despite them.

Workplace Resilience

Roffey Park Institute shares that "An organisation with strong team resilience is able to thrive whatever the wider world throws its way".

Organisations where leaders prioritise their people are the most resilient.

The Health and Safety Executive states that:

"There are six main areas that can lead to work-related stress if they are not managed properly. These are demands, control, support, relationships, role and change.

For example, workers may say that they:

- *are not able to cope with the demands of their jobs*

- *are unable to control the way they do their work*
- *don't receive enough information and support*
- *are having trouble with relationships at work, or are being bullied*
- *don't fully understand their role and responsibilities*
- *are not engaged when a business is undergoing change.*

Stress affects people differently; what stresses one person may not affect another. Factors like skills and experience, age or disability may all affect whether a worker can cope.”

They go on to add that by talking to your workers and understanding how to identify the signs of stress, you can prevent and reduce stress in your workplace.

These are all the reasons I continually talk about resilience in and out of the workplace. It’s so important in helping us to continually shape and influence a culture of well-being when we can demonstrate a resilient mindset and approach.

Resilience Superpowers

It’s important that we continue to build our everyday resilience, strengthening the attributes and qualities we have to help us progress. Ultimately, it’s about recognising and sharpening our practice, using our own internal superpowers.

In my lockdown research about resilience, I identified twenty tenets or dimensions that help people to be resilient. I refer to these as our Resilience Superpowers.

These are: Connection, Self-Belief, Drive, Focus, Organisation, Confidence, Awareness, Grit, Presence, Purpose, Energy, Influence, Values, Learning, Change, Perspective, Emotions, Self-Care, Optimism and Flexibility.

I am going to dive into the first eight to get you started.

There's a short definition for each, followed by some coaching questions that you can use as a self-coaching opportunity or to coach others within your team.

Connection

Ensuring that we have meaningful connections and supportive relationships in our lives, making genuine connections with people in whom we are happy to invest our time and collaborating with those people who make us feel good and vice versa, both in business and in life.

Ask yourself:

- When did you last have a meaningful conversation? What was it about? How did it help or impact? Who was it with?
- What (or who) are you negatively connecting to? Why? For what purpose?
- When do you need to disconnect? From what or whom? What steps can you take to address this?

- How are you building relationships with the people that matter to you?
- When, how and where are you currently networking? What networks have you not yet engaged with?

Self-Belief

To have confidence and trust in your own skills, abilities and judgement. It's the feeling that you have inside that you are capable of anything, fuelled with empowerment and strength. You can see opportunities and solutions and can cope with and move forward from setbacks.

Ask yourself:

- When and where have you believed in yourself? How did you demonstrate this? Who else noticed? How did believing in yourself help you?
- What are your self-limiting beliefs? How and when did you make the decision to believe these?
- When have these limiting beliefs been present?
- How will you dispute, disprove, and dispel limiting beliefs? If you continue to believe these, what will be the consequences?
- How will you begin to redress your limiting beliefs? What did you/will you do to counter them and focus on your positive beliefs?

Drive

Personal drive turns ideas into action and action into results. It keeps you going when it gets tough and it's the fuel to pursue, progress and achieve your goals. It's the perfect combination of desire to direct your energy towards what you set your heart and mind to.

Ask yourself:

- How do you keep going even when times are tough and challenging?
- When facing difficulty, how will you shift towards what can be done to put things right? How will you take this forward?
- How do your creative ideas and plans hold up in different scenarios and environments?
- What's the best possible outcome you can envision? How will you work towards this? What are the pros and cons of potential options?
- What would you do if you knew you couldn't fail?

Focus

To be intentional with what you focus your laser precision and attention on, be able to adjust the lens when clarity is required. It is in being able to choose carefully and knowing when to say, 'yes' or 'no'. When we are focused, our energy is channelled into that one direction, magnifying our efforts.

Ask yourself:

- What will you intentionally focus on today? What are you most excited about right now? What are you looking forward to?
- What are you currently focussing on? Where do you need to adjust your lens? Where or what are you wasting focus on?
- What are you looking for? Where will you find it? Where are you looking? (Is it to the past, present or future?)
- What clarity does understanding yourself bring to your personal and professional life?

Organisation

Being organised is one of the most effective skills in achieving success. Notice your success and failure triggers, being particularly careful to do things in bite-sized chunks whilst also mile-stoning progress. When we're organised, we have systems in place, we think more clearly, and we align with our targets and how we are going to reach them. Regular planning ensures we keep our priorities at the forefront and focus of our actions.

Ask yourself:

- What does 'being organised' mean to you?
- When you are organised, how does that make you feel? What does it look like? What happens when you are organised?

- How (dis) organised are you? Where are you (dis) organised? How is that helping/blocking your progress?
- What's currently on your to-do/priority list? How long has it been there for? When do you plan to have it crossed off?
- How are you organising your to-do list? What's on there that is not a priority?

Confidence

Linked to self-belief, confidence is the courage to know yourself, believe in yourself and act on your beliefs. Confidence can be situational, therefore it's not a fixed attribute, rather it's the outcome of the thoughts we think and the actions we take. Practice isn't about the progress to perfection, but it does make for consistent action.

Ask yourself:

- Where are you most confident? (Space, environment, location, situation, context)
- What are you doing, saying, feeling and hearing when you are confident? Who else notices this? What is achieved?
- When you are confident, what is the air like around you?
- When you are not your confident self? Where is this? Why is this? When is this? What's going on at that time?
- Who are you when you are confident? What happens?

Awareness

Self-awareness is a critical tool in helping you to reach higher levels of satisfaction, improve relationships and manage your emotions better. It's also positively correlated with higher levels of overall happiness. Being self-aware can help you align your current life with your passions.

Ask yourself:

- What do you know to be true about yourself? What do others know about you?
- How have you become you? What are you like? How do you know this?
- What's your message to yourself and the world? What does your internal dialogue say?
- What do you not know about yourself? (Ask others)
- How do you want others to see you? How would others describe you? How would you like to be described?

Grit

Grit can be likened to determination and is a positive emotional feeling that involves persevering towards a difficult goal despite obstacles. Having courage and conscientiousness can help, as well as further developing your follow-through to be a complete finisher in life and work.

- What does it mean to you to be determined? What are the benefits of being determined?
- How often do you give up on something? Why? How do you know when it's time to give up?
- How will you become more efficient in your use of determination and grit? What changes do you want to make to your life and environment?
- What is the hardest thing that you have ever done? How did you succeed? What is your intention for today, for this week, this month, this year?

Additional tool: You can download the eight Resilient Superpowers as a coaching card deck resource here. **www.dnacoach.co.uk/resilientminideck.**

Building Resilience Reserves

Look back at your results from earlier, when I asked you to consider what you are like when you are at your best and what you are like when you are not at your best. You will find that there will be elements in your responses that help you be more resilient and possibly things that are currently diluting/depleting your reserves.

Answering the questions from the eight resilient superpowers can help us build up our resilience reserves so that we can dip in and out of them as and when we need them.

Being able to support your team members during difficult times at work is paramount, as is supporting your people/teams' everyday needs, so they can show up and be at their best.

Understanding what motivates and engages your team members can help you to shape and influence their environment where they are best set up for success, as can learning and accepting that things don't always go the way we'd like on our first or even second time around.

Extra resource: Take this Resilience Reserves survey that I've built to help support you and your team members in identifying which of the eight resilience superpowers you have strength of reserves in, and which may need supercharging.

www.dnacoach.co.uk/resiliencereserves

Engage, Transform, Supercharge 'Resilience' Summary

Engage

Let's engage in cultivating a resilient mindset by creating a culture that values resilience as a priority, opening up with conversations about the importance of resilience in navigating the challenges and setbacks we face. Note that whilst we have reviewed superpowers here in a metaphorical way, we are not 'superhuman' and there will be times when we need a resilience boost.

Encourage your team members to share their experiences and insights on resilience by creating a psychologically safe and supportive environment where vulnerability is welcomed and learning opportunities are embraced.

Transform

Transforming our approach to resilience into more than just a pandemic and post-pandemic buzzword involves reframing challenges as opportunities for growth and learning. It's about shifting our mindset from seeing obstacles as roadblocks to viewing them as stepping stones to resilience.

As leaders and managers, lead by example by sharing what you have done in the face of adversity. Role model those strategies you have adopted, such as the use of reframing or proactive problem solving, and don't be afraid to seek support when it's needed and encourage others to do the same.

Supercharge

To supercharge our resilience efforts, we need to invest in appropriate resources and support systems that promote resilience, such as employee assistance programs, mental health resources and stress management workshops. And as I mentioned before, we can supercharge our efforts by fostering a culture of continuous learning and innovation. This involves encouraging experimentation and a little bit of supported risk-taking, not forgetting to embrace failures as valuable learning opportunities.

By creating a psychologically safe environment where individuals feel empowered to try new things and learn from mistakes, we supercharge resilience at an organisational level, underpinned by a growth mindset.

Overall, supporting resilience on an individual level involves practising self-care, setting boundaries and seeking help when needed. It's about recognising our own limitations and being kind to ourselves during difficult times.

As leaders and managers, we play a crucial role in supporting resilience in others by providing mentorship, encouragement and opportunities for growth. We foster a culture of empathy, where individuals feel safe to share their struggles and receive support from their peers and colleagues.

Let's Not Stop Here: keep the momentum going and refer to the Resilient Mindset Toolkit section in your downloadable workbook. Share it with your team and use this as an action plan to work on together.

www.dnacoach.co.uk/leadersassembleworkbook

I'll share with you how to practise a self-care mindset in a later chapter, but for now, grab yourself a cuppa and reflect. You've earned it.

REALISING THE COACH WITHIN

8
REALISING THE COACH WITHIN

How to Have Everyday Curious Coaching Conversations

I have been a coach for many years. In fact, I was coaching before I knew what coaching was. I'd describe myself as a naturally curious and inquisitive person, some might say nosey, and I love listening to what people have to say and hearing how they go about their day, make the decisions they do and why they do what they do.

I didn't do a formal coach training certification until 2013, and I've gone on to upgrade that every few years. I had previously taken part in many coach training programmes in the workplace and attended Association for Coaching masterclasses since 2008.

It was at an Association for Coaching masterclass event in Edinburgh that I met the wonderful Sir John Whitmore. I can't quite recall the year, but it must have been post-2008 as I remember him postulating the humorously provocative question, "Where were all the workplaces coaches when this was going on?" before giving the tongue-in-cheek response of "Oh yeah, nowhere as they had all been made redundant following the banking crisis". He was referencing the very blinkered and short-term view that many organisations have that when they are pressed for time, resources or budgets and looking to cut costs or save, it's usually the 'people departments', such as learning and development, that take the hit first.

I had intentionally booked that particular event to go along and meet John as I was already a fan after reading his book, *'Coaching for Performance'*, and being trained in how to use his GROW model framework in an earlier job.

I loved the effortless way he guided the Association for Coaching audience through how to use coaching in a way that wouldn't feel contrived or that coaching was something 'done' to you in the workplace.

He spoke about his way of thinking about coaching and his experience in the world of motor racing through to becoming a thought leader in the business world and leadership development. He spoke about his definition of coaching, about unlocking potential. Having read his book, I was already familiar with his definition of coaching as "unlocking potential to maximise performance", but there was something so special about hearing him talk about it in person, right in front of me.

The phrase 'unlocking potential' has stuck with me for that whole time. I use it as a mindset approach to remember that each and every one of us has potential and sometimes that potential is untapped or unrecognised, just sitting there waiting in the background ready to be brought out to the forefront. I think that this and the principles of a growth mindset align so well.

In that session, John spoke about his coaching framework, the GROW model, and its simplicity and flexibility, yet the powerful and profound impact it can have in unlocking that hidden or undiscovered potential.

This, to me, is one of the many reasons I adore everything that coaching brings. It's been such a game-changer for me over the years.

Coaching within organisations has so many benefits. It annoys me when I hear that coaching is only available to C-Suite leaders (the folks with 'Chief' in their job title) because coaching should be something available to everyone, at all levels. It shouldn't be something that is 'done to us'. It should be something that we can all curiously engage in, collaborate with and influence forward-focused change with.

In my business, DNA Coach, we created our own way of describing coaching, our own definition if you like and I always share it in every coach training programme I deliver (followed by Sir John's definition):

> Coaching is an everyday curious conversation to help people make change and move forward.

You might be reading that and thinking you've heard that somewhere before and you're right. You heard it right here, in this book, as I have weaved in the latter statement of 'make change and move forward' continuously throughout so far.

My cup of ambition, to channel my inner Dolly once again, is for everyone to not fear coaching. That might seem a bit of an odd statement, to fear coaching, but it comes from the feedback I have heard time and time again, and even from my own experiences, too. I've heard people report that coaching is only a practice that is wheeled in and wheeled out to solely address an underperformance. In some organisations, it is viewed as the 'naughty step' where the shared collective is that 'you've made a mistake' or 'didn't hit your targets', and the consequence of that is that you 'get some coaching'.

Of course, coaching can be used as a way to address any sense of underperformance, but it's also important to remember that coaching is a balanced approach and is also about unlocking potential, readdressing the aged perspective that it's only used as a disciplinary tool.

Take a sporting professional for example, pick your sporting person of choice. Let's go with some tennis pros such as Serena Williams, Roger Federer and so on. These are people at the top of their game, elite professionals, and guess what? They all have a coach. They probably have multiple coaches in fact, for different areas of their craft. And I bet those coaches are employed to continue helping those sporting professionals to do two things, well, three actually – to *make a change, move forward and be at their best.*

This is what the power of coaching can do.

It's not just for the sporting professionals. Coaching can be used for anything and anyone. I genuinely can't think of a time when coaching couldn't be used. It's versatile, adaptive and has great flexibility.

Your role as a leader or manager should be far removed from command-and-control styles and more of a Leader as Coach. You can do this by having those everyday curious conversations.

Now, I'd always recommend having some formal coaching training but as a powerful starting point, you can have coaching conversations by exercising those curiosity muscles, opening up to listen and asking some impactful and insightful questions with the aim of helping your coachee to make change and/or move forward.

I guarantee that you are likely already doing this, but perhaps not currently recognising this to be the case (which we will cover shortly).

You can coach and you can be coached. Coaching is not hierarchical. Coaching doesn't always have to be the leader or manager coaching a team member. It could be the other way around, too. It could also be a team member coaching another team member.

You can also self-coach, I do that a lot. You could have internal coaches, external coaches, or niche coaches for certain disciplines, for example, my bestie, Lucy Jacobs (hi, Lucy) is an Agile Coach (she's also a transformation coach). And remember, you can use coaching for a whole host of reasons, contexts, situations or scenarios.

I used coaching to get rid of my ex-husband.

I really did. I'm not joking. That and a good word with myself, haha. But I just wanted to use that shock factor statement to show you that you really can engage in coaching for a wide variety of events, personally and professionally.

You can use coaching for goal-setting, problem-solving, developing capability, improving or enhancing performance, preparing yourself/state/mindset, unlocking potential, moving forward, improving confidence, making change, increasing self-awareness, improving self-esteem, empowering people, providing support, getting clarity, making decisions and for diagnostic uses.

It can also be helpful for times when you or another person might feel overwhelmed or frustrated, or if you are procrastinating, undecided or stuck on something, if you want to understand a perspective, or to make peace with or to let go of something. Perhaps there's a time when you recognise something needs to change or you want to get started on something or evaluate and assess a current situation where coaching can be used. Maybe you want to stop something, or you find yourself faced with a challenge or want to become accountable for something.

In all of these situations, you can coach someone (or yourself) to make a change and move forward. That's the power of coaching and what it can help you and others achieve.

Opening Up a Coaching Conversation

To start a coaching conversation, listen out for cues and clues that people give in conversation. Genuinely, most informal coaching conversations come from an around-the-kettle or a hallway chat – the ones where you are chewing the fat, having a chinwag and you ask someone how their day is and, low and behold, they actually tell you, rather than giving the stock answer of "It's been fine thanks, and yours?"

Some of the best coaching conversations I have had (in both roles of coach and coachee) have come from a blurt out, a rant or a divulge of information. The answer to the " How's your day been?" question is responded to with something like,

"Oh, terrible. I have a big deadline due Friday and two people are on holiday."

These little nuggets that people share can have a big impact. No doubt, as a good human being your 'go to' response here is most likely to acknowledge what your colleague has said and then ask a few questions. My instinct goes to these questions:

- Talk me through it. How can I help?
- Where are you in relation to the completion of the work to meet the deadline?
- Who else can assist?
- What options or ideas do you have?
- What else can you pause on for now to give you some space to meet the deadline?

You might have had similar things pop to the forefront of your mind. This can be an example of an everyday coaching conversation.

Informal and Formal Coaching Differences

In all workplace coach training programmes, I ask the following questions and give the options to choose from. Take a minute to answer them for yourself:

How often do you coach a member of your team?

- Daily
- Every few days
- Weekly
- Every few weeks
- Monthly

- Less frequent than monthly (i.e., quarterly)

This isn't a trick question to catch anyone out or to be clever; it's useful to help us recognise when we currently see opportunities to coach.

If you selected daily or every few days, this would likely suggest that you are having those everyday curious conversations on the hoof, as it were, the ones that naturally and spontaneously come up from a blurt out or a rant.

If you said weekly, every few weeks or monthly, this would likely suggest that you are having coaching conversations that are perhaps 'booked in'. Maybe from a weekly check-in meeting or a monthly one-to-one/performance review.

If you said less frequent than monthly, i.e., quarterly, this would likely suggest that this is more of an appraisal-style session, perhaps to plan objectives for the next quarter and to review performance.

So, the daily and every few days style of coaching is more of the informal coaching conversations (perhaps even the weekly ones are more of a check-in style) and those that are every few weeks, monthly and quarterly are likely to be the more sit-down formal ones where you might document conversations as part of your HR processes or performance management structure.

To be clear, all of these are needed, but what we do need to ensure we do is to balance the informal and formal coaching sessions within the workplace. I guarantee, that even if you didn't select daily or every few days, you will definitely be having these conversations but just didn't recognise them as coaching... until now.

Being Leader and Coach Combined

Herminia Ibarra and Anne Scoular, in their 2019 article in Harvard Business Review, put it perfectly:

"The coaching we're talking about — the kind that creates a true learning organisation — is ongoing and executed by those inside your organisation. It's work that all leaders and managers should engage in with all their people, all the time, in ways that help define the organisation's culture and advance its mission. An effective manager or leader as coach asks questions instead of providing answers, supports employees instead of judging them, and facilitates their development instead of dictating what has to be done."

They go on to add:

"Coaching is no longer just a benevolent form of sharing what you know with somebody less experienced or less senior, although that remains a valuable aspect. It's also a way of asking questions so as to spark insights in the other person."

Once again, we probably need another full book to support the topic of coaching overall (I've added that to my list of things to do) but in the meantime, let me share with you two coaching models to help you on your way to becoming the Leader as Coach.

The GROW Model

I thoroughly recommend you read Sir John Whitmore's *Coaching for Performance* book, (sadly, Sir, John passed away in 2017). It's one of the books I give out from time to time on my coach training programmes and qualifications, it's that good. In it, you'll learn so much more about the GROW model than the overview I will share here, but I promise what I do share will set you up for successful coaching conversations.

The GROW Model is my favourite of the coaching models after my own coaching model, which is coming up next, and it's probably the most globally known and used coaching model.

It's a simple and effective conversational coaching framework in the form of the GROW mnemonic, which is **Goal**, **Reality**, **Options** and **Will**. You may see the W sometimes represented as the **Way Forward** too.

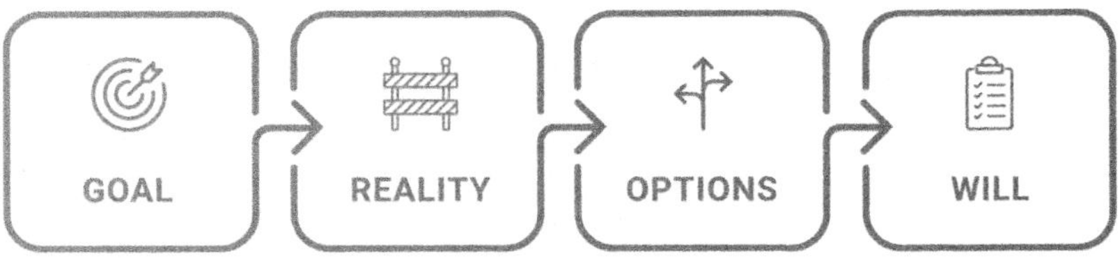

It can be used in a linear fashion, starting with Goal, then moving through Reality, then Options and closing your coaching conversation on the Will stage. It can also be used flexibly, depending on where the conversation perhaps starts or the direction it goes. For example, I often start a coaching conversation in the Reality space with a question like "What's on your mind?" or "What have you been up to since I saw you last?"

Let's go through it as the mnemonic reads:

Goal

This is the goal your coachee has in mind, one that they might present with straight away i.e., my goal is to write a book and have it published this calendar year.

It could be the goal that your team member has in their time with you i.e., what they'd like to get out of your time together and that could be as simple as 'gaining clarity'.

They can be short-, mid- or long-term goals... i.e., what they want to achieve today or this week or month, what they have as a target to hit in the next few months or what ambition they would like to realise this year, in three years, or even ten years.

Reality

This is where you help your coachee or team member explore where they are right now in their current situation in relation to what their goal might be. Maybe your team member's goal is to get a promotion this year or to achieve their best-ever customer experience targets this quarter. This is where you spend the time to help your coachee share where they are now in relation to that goal.

Options

This is the part of the conversation where you aid your coachee through insightful questions to identify the options they have available to them to help them unlock that potential and realise that ambition.

What ideas do they have that would help them to make that change or to move them forward? What could be a helpful course of action to take and what might they consider doing (or not doing)?

Will

This is the decision and action planning part of the conversation involving the 'will' to take those actions forward.

From the earlier discussion and the things your coachee has identified, what will they do? What's their first step? How confident and committed do they feel in taking those actions?

For example, they might need to go and locate the job description for the next role level or have some interview prep. This is also where you will agree with your coachee on any follow-ups to check in on progress and to help them stay accountable.

And that is how easy it is to implement an everyday curious coaching conversation.

How long should a coaching conversation last, I hear you ask. You can have coaching conversations in as little as ten minutes. It could be a one-off on a particular topic, or you could have a longer and more detailed conversation of thirty minutes, an hour, or even ninety minutes. I would personally limit ninety-minute sessions as the absolute maximum for workplace coaching.

Depending on the nature of what your coachee has on their mind or what they'd like coaching support with, timings, duration and frequency can vary.

Here are a few examples of great coaching questions for each of the GROW stages:

Goal

- What would you like to achieve longer-term/today/next half-hour?
- What will it look like when it's solved/as good as it can be?
- What area of your life/work would you like to focus on?
- What would you like to discuss?
- What would you like to get out of this session/these sessions?
- What do you want to have/be/do?
- What's your goal and what does that look like?
- What will that enable you to do?

Reality

- What is happening at the moment?
- Where are you now in relation to your goal?
- How important is this to you?
- What is holding you back?
- How much control do you have over the situation?
- What/which is the biggest blocker and how do you/will you get around it?
- What are you doing that takes you towards your goal?
- What are you doing that is getting in the way of your goal?

Options

- What could you do?
- What ideas do you have?
- What alternatives do you have?
- Is there anything else? If there were anything else, what would it be?
- What has worked in the past?
- What steps could you take?
- Who could help you with this?
- Where could you find out the information?
- What other angles can you think of?

Will

- What is to be done, when, and by whom?
- Which option/s will you choose?

- What actions will you take and when?
- What is the next step?
- When will you start?
- When will you have achieved your goal?
- When will you review that/your progress?
- How will you track your progress?

Having this curious approach to conversations, where, as a leader, you are refraining from solving the other person's problem for them, allows people space to pause and ponder on what they could do to make that change and move forward, pouncing into purposeful action.

The Coaching Mindset

Coaching starts with your mindset. The International Coaching Federation outlines the Coaching Mindset as one of its key foundational competencies to become an effective coach. They believe that all coaches should adopt and embody a coaching mindset – this can be defined as being able to develop and maintain a mindset that is open, curious, flexible and client or people-centred.

At DNA Coach, we ask leaders, managers and coaches to adopt a coaching mindset approach. You can do this by keeping the statements below at the forefront of your mind. Like a set of mantras or beliefs that you should hold about your coachee or your team member that will enable a more empowering coaching relationship:

- Maximise the coachee's potential by allowing the coachee to unlock their own answers (where possible)
- Believe that there is excellence in every one of us
- Enhance the coachee's ability to think about new possibilities, actions and outcomes
- Promote well-being and support and aid motivation
- Listen deeply and without judgement or assumption (be blame-free)
- Encourage action that reaches toward a goal after each coaching session
- Promote accountability by enabling the coachee to identify concrete actions and potential setbacks
- Promote awareness and responsibility and encourage self-belief in your coachees
- Build trust and aid a solutions focus
- Ethically challenge, engage, encourage, support and motivate
- Aid your coachee in grounding solutions in the reality of their day-to-day work.

Leader as Coach Quiz: This short self-assessment survey is to assess yourself against some key coaching principles, where you will receive some feedback on your coaching approach and style along with some recommendations, too.

www.dnacoach.co.uk/coachapproachquiz

The DNA Coaching Model

Another useful coaching model, created by me and using my company values is The DNA (Develop & Define, Nurture & Engage, Apply & Achieve) Coaching Model.

It's useful here to bring ourselves back to the belief that coaching is and should be at the very centre of your business and as consistent as your DNA.

Imagine a workplace where coaching conversations happen every single day, where it is not something that is solely used as a performance management tool, wheeled in and out to correct issues or underperformance.

It's the very values of our DNA model approach that ensure we start taking coaching seriously in the workplace and integrating its daily application to promote a successful and winning mindset. Just like we've said before, top athletes and sports people have coaches (sometimes more than one) to help them be at their best, even when they are already doing pretty well or at the peak of their game. Coaching for them is habitual and as consistently natural as every breath you take.

Our workplaces need more coaches. We need our business leaders to operate from both positions of leader and coach.

Some common myths that stop coaching from becoming the norm in the workplace are:

Common myth #1
"I just don't have time to coach"

Let's break that first one down. I guarantee that you coach already, but don't realise it. You don't always need to have lengthy ninety-minute or longer sessions to coach someone. Coaching in the workplace can be as straightforward as a conversation, or a series of short conversations with a purpose. The purpose is to unlock potential, make change or move forward.

Common myth #2
"I don't have the skills to coach"

It's my mission to ensure that coach training is accessible for everyone in the workplace, not just the big wigs with the big titles. The first step is to connect with your coachee, listen to them and recognise if they are open to having a coaching conversation. Be curious and ask some great questions to elicit some more information from the coachee about where they are and where they'd like to be. Ask questions that stretch their thinking towards potential.

As a great coach, you need to listen carefully and create the space for the coachee, and with your coaching support, help them create an action plan that will move them forward.

To help with this, the DNA of the Coaching Model has been created and designed to be short, sweet, simple and straightforward, to help you guide your coachee conversations.

You can use the following as a self-coaching tool or to enable great coaching conversations:

DEVELOP & DEFINE

The Develop & Define questions are 'intent focused'.

Framed on an awareness of what you want to have, be or do, ultimately, what is it that you want to develop?

These questions help you create an awareness of where things are now and where you'd like to shift that to. This helps focus your attention and gives you greater clarity.

Here are some great questions to help you or your coachee develop that awareness.

- What's on your mind? What's happening right now?
- What area would you like to focus on?
- What do you want to strengthen, balance, enhance, improve, change, resolve or develop?

- What would you like to have happen?
- What would you like to have more of/less of?
- What would make the biggest difference?
- What result or outcome are you looking for?
- What is your ambition/ideal situation?

NURTURE & ENGAGE

The Nurture & Engage questions tap into the ecology of why you do what you do.

Aligning to your purpose and when you have that nailed, you become engaged in it; you're fully committed, aligned with your values and 'all in'. You create engagement when a vision ignites a passion. This is about engaging your heart, mind, soul, hands and spirit in whatever your goal is.

Here are some questions to get you engaged in your goal and to know what stirs that spirit and drives engagement. It also helps to recognise what's stopping you and allows you to start making progress to work through that.

- What are you doing that's moving you forward?
- What about this excites and inspires you?
- What are you doing that is getting in the way of your goal?
- How important is this to you and the people around you?
- What impact will it have for you to achieve this/your goal?
- What has stopped you from getting it/there so far?
- What needs to change?

- What might you need to say no to?
- How could you turn this around, starting today?
- Imagine three months from now, all obstacles are removed, and you have achieved this: What do you see/hear/feel? What new elements are in place? What is different?

APPLY & ACHIEVE

Motivation is the key driving effort and differential in progress (and not perfection).

I want you to fully commit to what you want to achieve by engaging with it and being motivated to action. This is where we combine that intrinsic and extrinsic motivation and splash in a good dash of effort to get there.

Here are some questions to help you and your coachee make a plan that sticks, based on progress and not perfection.

- What is your first manageable step?
- What are one-three actions that you can take to get started this week?
- What would happen if you did nothing? (Positive or negative)
- How will you counter this?
- How will you put your options together to form a plan?
- How motivated/committed are you to this plan?
- How will you prepare for that?

- What are the progress milestones you can track along the way?
- Who are the key people in your network to support?
- How will you measure your success?

Coaching PDF Tool: These questions are part of a handy coaching card downloadable PDF. You can access it here - www.dnacoach.co.uk/dnacard

When 'Fine' Doesn't Mean Fine

I want to address the response that many of us make when asked the question "How are you?".

The "How are you?" question is a great coaching opener, as well as an everyday conversation starter, but I'd like you to truly listen and observe the responses, especially the "I'm fine" ones.

For the most part, people may actually be 'fine', which is great. But observing any subtleties or nuances of how this is delivered, listening to vocal patterns and tones and noting any accompanying facial expression response or posture shift, could be an opportunity to take that extra care and attention to spend a few more minutes checking in with your colleague or team member to ensure they are actually fine.

A really helpful way to do this is to follow up their "I'm fine" response with something like...

"Great to hear, what does fine look like for you?" or

"Lovely, how does fine show up for you?"

Of course, adding a caveat here, this should be asked in a non-contrived sounding way, with genuine curiosity.

There's a funny demonstration of the "I'm fine" response from the TV show Friends where the character Ross finds out about Joey and Rachel's relationship. His use of the word fine highlights that, in fact, Ross is not fine. You can find the clip online on YouTube or similar services.

In the clip you hear Joey reply with a "Really?" response, highlighting the important need, for our purposes here, to be careful with our expression of response, without sounding judgemental, ensuring that any response we have has a positive intent of checking-in to learn if the person is indeed fine, or they could do with a good chat.

Not Every Conversation Needs to be a Coaching Conversation

A short cautionary warning that sometimes coaching isn't the thing that is required. There may be occasions when a person is pressed for time or truly stuck or lacking in knowledge and they may need something else at that moment - some friendly advice, a suggestion or training perhaps. There will also be times when you need to provide an answer or response. This is why I had the bracketed caveat of **'where possible'** following the mindset approach of maximising the coachee's potential by allowing the coachee to unlock their own answers.

This should be the exception and not the norm. If you find yourself constantly in 'tell' mode, directing or spoon-feeding answers, then maybe there is an opportunity here for you to consider how you can redress that balance.

Self-Coaching

I am a big fan of self-coaching, I do it all the time. There are not many things I do these days or decisions I make without running it through a self-coaching conversation with myself. I do this using the GROW or the DNA model.

This is where coaching can be particularly useful to help in the everyday. I know if I am feeling overwhelmed with too much on my plate it can be quite debilitating for me and that can lead to me becoming anxious or frustrated. I might then procrastinate because I don't know where to start.

Being able to self-coach has made a massive difference to the approaches I've taken and the decisions I've made over the years. It's helped me be organised and purposeful, make clarity-based decisions, make peace and let go of some stuff along the way, too.

Why not try it out for yourself?

Use the coaching questions as prompts. Try journaling your responses if it feels a bit odd to think of them or to say them out loud. It's a great self-reflection and self-development habit to get into.

Ok, we have covered A LOT in this chapter (whole book coming on it next, I feel) so here is a short Engage, Transform and Supercharge summary to close this chapter off.

Engage, Transform, Supercharge 'Coaching' Summary

Engage

Coaching conversations start with you, as the Leader as Coach, demonstrating genuine curiosity and actively listening to your interactions. Show genuine interest in team members' experiences, goals and challenges, and encourage them to explore and reflect on their thoughts and feelings.

By engaging in curious coaching conversations, we foster a culture of learning, growth, and innovation.

Transform

Your approach to coaching conversations shifts from a persistent directive mindset to a curious mindset. It's about reframing our role as coaches from problem solvers to facilitators of growth and self-discovery. Instead of providing answers, ask thought-provoking questions that challenge assumptions, stimulate reflection and spark creativity.

We encourage experimentation, exploration and learning from failure, rather than seeking quick fixes or solutions.

Supercharge

With our curious coaching conversations, we need to integrate curiosity into every aspect of our leadership by embedding it into our feedback practices, performance reviews and evaluations and any talent development initiatives, providing opportunities for peer-to-peer coaching and mentoring, where team members can learn from each other and exchange insights and perspectives.

Ultimately the key takeaway is that coaching should become part of your everyday culture.

Let's Not Stop Here: keep the momentum going and refer to the DNA of Coaching Toolkit section in your downloadable workbook. Share it with your team and use this as an action plan to work on together.

www.dnacoach.co.uk/leadersassembleworkbook

REVOLUTIONISING REVIEWS

9
REVOLUTIONISING REVIEWS

Reviewing How We Review

I might be in the minority here, but I always loved my performance reviews or appraisals, with the exception of that one time with poor Stewart when I cried a lot. Not because I was always good at my job and they were a breeze. I had many reviews, one-to-ones and appraisals where feedback was shared on performance and a discussion took place on what I would take forward.

Maybe, in some sense, I have been lucky as overall, with the exception of one or two utterly horrible dictators (I mean directors), leaders or managers, I have been blessed by working with and for many exceptional people.

I enjoyed the process and the experience of discussing where I am now, what led me to this point and what comes next. And if the truth be told, the questions from that one sentence are exactly what a performance review discussion should be:

Where are you now?
What led you to this point?
And what's next?

Performance Reviews have been getting a bad rap for years, with many companies even moving away from appraisals and review structures as they feel too rigid or present bias, and instead favouring the things I have spoken about in the book so far, such as providing a culture of psychological safety, learning, growth, and helpful and future-focused feedback, with curious coaching conversations and so forth.

Annual appraisals or any review practice that feels formal and fussy or has scorings attached to it can feel restrictive.

Yet reviews and appraisals don't have to become obsolete. We just need to change the way they happen.

Let's stop referring to them as a process or a box-ticking exercise. Instead, let's make it an empowering and inspiring experience where people are supported to make progress, develop, make change and move forward.

I'm certainly not going to dictate that you should scrap your performance management system or appraisal process and start again. Rather, I ask you to reframe how that is positioned in the organisation as an aid to a person's personal and professional development and not something to metaphorically beat a person with.

So, call the time that you spend here whatever you feel fits best: performance review, performance conversation, one-to-one discussion, appraisal, employee evaluation, annual or mid-year review or check-in. Let's work towards removing the stigma that it comes with, that naughty step that we conjure in our minds, and instead, embrace it as something positive and helpful to look forward to. View it as an enabler.

My two personal favourite terms for this type of time spent are a Career Conversation or a Growth Review.

I think there is room for everyday coaching conversations, weekly check-ins, monthly one-to-ones, quarterly and annual appraisals etc., as long as they are both career and growth-focused, conversational and allow time to reflect.

The only thing I would ever suggest as an absolute minimum requirement is that there should always be at least one booked-in-the-calendar and immovable monthly catch-up every single month, without fail. This would fall within the more 'formal' style that we discussed in the previous chapter.

The Review in Review

Question: What should we review in a review? (still calling it that for the purpose of the chapter overall)

Answer: As much as you can around the entire person.

Find out what a team member's drivers are. What motivates them to come to work? Why this job and company? What do they want from their role? What do they want to feel at the end of a working day or week? What are their needs, wants, aspirations and desires? What do they enjoy about what they do and what do they not? What one thing would they like to try out or change? How do they view their role and contribution? How do they feel they are performing? What would they benefit from? What's on their workplace bucket list (another personal fave)? What's their passion? What motivates them outside of work? Where would they like to develop and progress or improve upon? As always, the list is endless.

We can find out the answers to all of those questions with the three overarching ones from earlier:

Where are you now?
What led you to this point?
And what's next?

Scored Reviews - Marks Out of Ten?

I give it a 5/10 – just kidding.

Or am I? Actually, I feel on the fence about scoring performance reviews and evaluations, where we attribute ratings to things like measures, targets and objectives or how a person demonstrated the company values.

These can be so subjective, open to bias such as favouritism etc, and open to misinterpretation or disagreement on what differentiates a score of five against a score of four, for example.

The manager scores the team member, the team member scores themselves, they both sit down and agree or disagree, pieces of paper are filled in and submitted to HR or filed in the employee records folder, never to be seen again until it's whipped out again to compare against on the next review.

This is the part that always feels a bit of a drag and perhaps a wasted effort.

We should be having growth reviews because they have a purpose. They help you and the team member shape the plan of action based on learnings and ambitions, where you map out the timeline, milestones and progress checks along the way.

And, if I am being truly honest… I'd much rather have a 'performance appraisal' that's rated with an even more simple scale:

- **Did this happen, yes or no? (Or nearly)**
- **Either way, what's next?**

Maybe that's too simplistic a viewpoint but I am a fan of not overcomplicating things for the sake of it.

Instead, let's revolutionise those reviews so that team members can RISE.

The RISE Framework

Revolutionising the way reviews are perceived and performed with the DNA Coach RISE Framework changes how you harness them and your people's perspective of them, creating a space where feedback, self-reflection, support and guidance empower your people, provides innovative thinking and where the contribution of every team member is highly and positively valued.

Recognise and Reflect

As a leader, it's important to recognise the contributions of your people, as we discussed in the recognition chapter. Encourage colleagues to reflect on their areas of passion and interest and engage in open, honest reflections about past experiences, successes and any challenges.

Encourage team members to reflect on their performance, share insights gained from their experiences and discuss strategies for improvement moving forward.

Individualise and Inspire

This focuses on the individual person and *their* goals, *their* achievements and where they might like some additional support, along with ensuring you provide the resources to enable this to happen. This then creates an inspirational way to focus your people's attention for a powerful and positive impact. Recognise that each team member is unique and has different strengths, areas of focus and goals.

Tailor conversations to focus on individual growth and development rather than that one-size-fits-all approach.

Self-Directed and Strengths-Based

Remember to continue creating a culture of coaching and support where you are the Leader as Coach, mentor even, rather than acting as an evaluator. Provide guidance, encouragement and resources to help team members continue towards success. Equally, encourage conversations to guide team members to create their own growth plans, based on their strengths and career goals.

Encourage colleagues to take ownership of their development by setting their own objectives, identifying learning opportunities and seeking feedback from others, rather than spoon-feeding every objective.

Empowerment and Ownership

Yes, of course, there will be company goals that may not have a lot of wiggle room or negotiation but get your team members engaged in it as early as possible. Empower team members to take ownership of their performance and career development.

Encourage self-assessment, reflection and even autonomy and authority to make decisions related to their work.

Engage, Transform and Supercharge Review Summary

Engage

Revolutionising reviews should be a collaborative opportunity for growth and development, rather than a one-sided evaluation.

Engage team members through conversation.

Transform

Our approach to reviews needs to move away from traditional, top-down evaluation towards a more transformative conversational style.

Consider making reviews more frequent with ongoing feedback conversations that are focused on growth and development.

Supercharge

Let's supercharge our efforts in revolutionising reviews and foster a culture of continued recognition and appreciation. It's about celebrating achievements and milestones, both big and small, **throughout the whole year**.

Acknowledge and appreciate efforts and contributions regularly, rather than waiting for an annual review or appraisal.

Let's Not Stop Here: keep the momentum going and refer to the Revolutionising Reviews Toolkit section in your downloadable workbook. Share it with your team and use this as an action plan to work on together.

www.dnacoach.co.uk/leadersassembleworkbook

ENGAGED ACTION PLANNING

10
ENGAGED ACTION PLANNING

Moving From Goal-Setting to Goal-Getting

I encourage people to set goals (and get) goals often and not just at the turning point of the calendar year. Many folks these days can seem quite averse to the new year resolution setting as a little bit gimmicky. The whole 'new year new you' phenomenon can sometimes feel like it only applies to when you want to 'quit drinking' or to 'get fitter' etc, and yet the act of goal setting or intention/resolution setting can be super powerful for those examples like 'quitting the booze' and 'getting fit,' as well as a whole host of other things too.

We actually set goals every single day and don't really think about it. Your alarm clock time, the time you need to leave the house, or when you need to log into teams or Zoom, work through your to-do list, your tasks and activities, getting to an evening class, getting to bed by a set time, planning the summer holiday, saving up to buy something, studying for an exam, working towards a promotion...all of which are your everyday 'type' of goals. We set them consistently and regularly.

As leaders and managers, we can support this practice in the workplace by having those regular growth reviews and check-ins with our team members to support them in whatever it is they are working on – whether that be the 'day job' activities or the stretch stuff in support of progression, learning or development.

You can successfully use conversational coaching models like GROW, and the DNA of Coaching model to help set goals, and there are a number of other popular frameworks available such as SMART (specific, measurable, achievable, relevant, time-bound) or OKRs (objectives and key results).

Moving From Goal-Setting to Goal-Getting

Setting goals is a great way to recalibrate your life and work plans on a regular basis. It's an opportunity to do an inventory – where do you currently stand and where would you like to be? The only way you'll maintain control of where you're going is by setting goals or resolutions.

There are three directions in which you are moving (or not) – forwards, backwards or standing still. I believe the latter is the same as moving backwards when it comes to goals. Why? Because time continues to move forward. Always be determined to give everything your best to improve your chances – that means shifting from a **goal-setter to a goal-getter**.

Now, the reason many people may fail at New Year resolutions is that often, an intention is set but a plan is not put in place, or we're not fully engaged or committed. Sometimes, other stuff gets in the way and sometimes, we decide that actually, that isn't the thing you want to be focused on right now, after all.

> Getting fully engaged in our goals is the way forward.

We need to not just set a goal, but we need to formulate a plan of action to go and get that goal. This could include doing a bit of research, carving out time in your schedule to work on your goal, mapping out what progress and success would look like for you and identifying a suitable time frame overall, including the milestones and check-in points along the way.

How we set and get goals doesn't have to be that different, if at all different, in or outside of the workplace.

Setting goals and achieving them can seem overwhelming, but the thing about goals is that they're just like navigating our way to a destination. When you plan a trip to somewhere you've never been before, you plot the journey, maybe work out alternative routes and ensure your means of transport is appropriate. This is all simply to be able to achieve your aim of reaching your goals. There has never been a more important time for your organisation to be people-centred and believe me when I tell you that coaching IS the way forward to achieve this.

I encourage all business leaders and individuals to move forward, to use learnings from the past and to help people shift their focus towards the future. Ask yourself and your colleagues, what is it that you want to have happen and what actions can you take today to start making small steps towards progress?

Take action: We are going to start with you and your goals, some self-coaching and some action planning. Work through this for yourself first and you will see how and where you can support others in this too.

Think of a goal you have. It could be a life goal or a work goal, you can even choose one of each. It might be something you've always wanted to have, be or do... maybe a bucket list item, or an ambition, something you'd like to achieve. It can be anything at all.

Note it down *and write it out in whatever way springs to mind.*

Here are a few examples:

- I'd like to become a published author (or even simpler, I'd like to write a book)
- I want to be better organised
- I'd like to get a promotion at work
- I'd like to learn how to do advanced Excel formulas, to be an Excel expert

- I want to take my family abroad on holiday this year
- I'd like to be able to get to the gym twice a week
- I'd like to wake up each morning without having five 'snooze' alarms go off before I finally get out of bed
- I'd like to complete a qualification that leads towards a professional membership to help me in my role
- I'd like to pay off my credit card this year
- I want to successfully meet and exceed my targets every single month without feeling overwhelmed
- I'd like to become a workplace coach or mentor
- I want to sign up to do the London Marathon
- I'd like to get involved in charitable activities in my community

Whatever your goal is, or your team member's goal is, spending time detailing and mapping it out can have significantly higher progress and success rates than just stating it alone. Identifying a want, need or desire is your first step.

When working on organisational goals and objectives, it's important that you share in the vision of that, as a leader or manager, to help connect the organisational dots to a colleague's involvement and contribution, rather than dictating what must be completed.

Either way, you need to get engaged in the goal. So, let's use our ENGAGE model to help you do just that.

Let's ENGAGE

So, how do we set goals and stick to them? How do you achieve the change or the success that you want? With a robust action plan. Action plans help to break a project into small and defined tasks, and it is often the thing we forget to commit to or follow because we are so consumed solely by 'what the goal is' rather than 'why it's important' and 'how you get there'.

Developing an action plan clarifies goals to be achieved, teams and service providers to be involved, tasks, dependencies, milestones and resources needed to complete the project. Action plans also help track progress and measure project performance. Action plans prepare you for predictable and preventable challenges that focus your resources, enabling you to achieve your main goals.

The ENGAGE model is to Envision, Notice, Gather, Action Plan, Get Help and Gain Momentum, then Evaluate and Track.

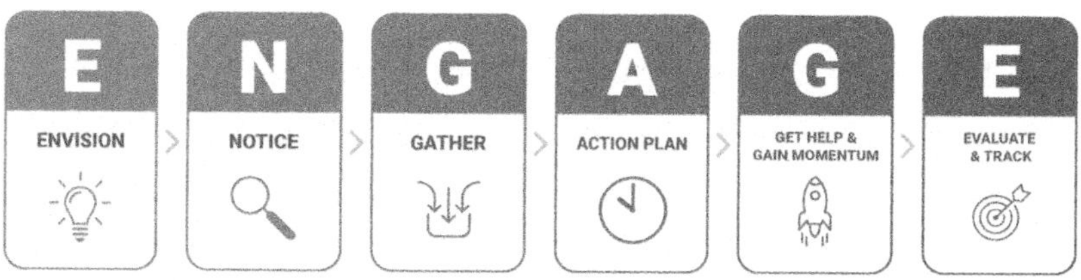

Envision

Never to be underestimated is the power of visualisation, so, start by describing what your goal is and what that looks like for you once you've achieved it.

The key here is to give as much detail into the future state of obtaining your goal as you possibly can.

Also, dig deep into the 'why' behind your goal. Why do you want this? What will it bring you (and others)? Why is it important?

Think about yourself in the future having completed it or attained it. What will be different? How will this benefit you?

Notice

This is where you explore the reality of now as an opportunity to reflect. Notice where you are now in relation to your goal. What has led you to today?

Assess the current situation, reflect on the progress made so far and what's still to come. Notice what you haven't achieved...yet.

The power of **yet** is crucial here. Understand what has perhaps stopped you so far. Where are there any blockers, actual or perceived? We always feel we've never got enough time and resources, so this is important to reflect here and to consider that if progress isn't being made, then the picture we envisioned will never come to fruition.

Gather

This is where we get into some thinking and detail.

How will you reach your goals?

Be realistic about how you'll achieve your goals and what your options are. Keep it simple and consider how you'll navigate any changes or bumps along the road should they arise.

This is your fact-finding mission to identify and gather the possibilities, options and alternatives.

What information do you need? What's missing? What potential is available here?

Action Plan

This is where we plot the journey with the action plan.

Time is of the essence, so it's prudent to plan your time frame along with your milestones and actionable steps. What is your first step and when will this happen?

Map out how you're going to get to your goal. You'll need to decide what timeframe you're going to work towards, what milestones you'll be aiming for, what your first steps will look like and WHEN, not if, you're going to make this happen.

Get Help, Gain Momentum

In this part, you are getting and gaining (the double G).

Getting engaged applies to the right mindset – getting people involved, getting the learning done and getting going towards your goals.

Ready, set, get!!

Now that you have completed the first step, what are you doing now and next? Build that momentum through reflecting, learning and staying engaged by taking further actionable steps (even teeny tiny ones).

Don't be afraid to enlist the help of others in order to get you there, be that through your organisational peers, business employees or another member of your team. For life goals, that might be a pal or a loved one.

We cannot possibly do all the things by ourselves, all the time. It's perfectly okay to ask for help.

Evaluate and Track

This is about continued progress towards success. Commit to your plan and avoid becoming undone by distractions and shiny objects.

Ask yourself: How will I track and measure progress and success? How will I evaluate any lack of progress along the way? And how will I know when I have achieved my goal?

This is where it can be incredibly useful to journal about your journey to reach your goals, which not only offers clarity but also aids focus and presents an opportunity to reflect and most importantly, guides you towards reaching your goal.

I've created a one-page action plan document with space for you to note down your goal, identify your starting point of where you are now and then space for up to three action points to be documented with dates set, followed by a 'pit stop' to check-in on what you have achieved so far.

You can download and access it here:
www.dnacoach.co.uk/engagedactionplan

Time now for a short Engage, Transform and Supercharge summary.

Engage, Transform and Supercharge 'Goal Setting' Summary

Engage

It's about creating a sense of excitement and enthusiasm around the goals we set, inspiring everyone to contribute their ideas and efforts towards achieving them. By fostering a sense of belonging and involvement, we ensure that everyone feels invested in the success of the goals and committed to taking action to make them a reality.

Start with creating a shared vision and purpose. Then use the process of moving from goal-setting to goal-getting.

Transform

The approach from goal-setting to goal-getting is about shifting from passive planning or vague intention-setting to active implementation. It's about translating goals into actionable, measurable steps and developing concrete action plans to achieve them. Encouraging a culture of accountability and responsibility, where team members take ownership of their goals and are empowered to take decisive action.

Coaching, supporting colleagues and overcoming obstacles assist team members in staying focused on their goals.

Supercharge

Success in goal-getting comes from building on that motivation and momentum, celebrating progress and milestones along the way, recognising achievements and successes and of course, helping yourself and others view any setbacks as opportunities for growth. It's about learning where it's okay to redefine, tweak and reshape rather than giving up.

We can choose to view obstacles as part of the pathway to success.

Let's Not Stop Here: keep the momentum going and refer to the Engaged Action Planning Toolkit section in your downloadable workbook. Share it with your team and use this as an action plan to work on together.

www.dnacoach.co.uk/leadersassembleworkbook

EDGE TOWARDS CHANGE

11

EDGE TOWARDS CHANGE

Navigating Workplace Change

Imagine how you might feel if you were standing on a lovely fluffy rug which very quickly gets pulled out from underneath your feet without a moment's notice. It could conjure up all manner of feelings and responses, which is why, well-managed, coached and communicated change can help us to navigate our path forward with far better outcomes.

Change is constant and how we deal with change can vary depending on the type of change it is, our feelings around it, the beliefs we hold and whether we've had any influence or say in the change itself or have made the decision directly. Sometimes, change happens to us, in terms of being bestowed or forced upon us. Sometimes, change is something we actively seek out as a way to progress, move forward or innovate.

Of course, some change is positive, and some will be negative, depending on a whole host of circumstances. We need to be prepared for change as best we can. But sometimes, we don't foresee the change until it lands right at our feet. Sometimes, it comes as a complete curveball so we don't have any time to prepare for it, we just need to deal with it, there and then, as best we can, or manage the consequences and ripple effects of that change.

The power of adaptability and resilience is key to being able to manage any change that occurs and being 'change ready'.

Once again, we deal with change all of the time, quite successfully - changes to schedules, direction and seasons, so I know you can manage future change when it arises.

Being able to support yourself through change and, in turn, support others, will aid a smoother transition towards any change you or your colleagues might face.

Learning exercise: Think of some examples of workplace change that you have faced already.

Note them down.

Capture your thoughts around those changes. How was it communicated? Were you involved in the decision or change process? How was the change received by you and others? What was the outcome of the change? How did you feel about it and how did you respond (or react)? What was the wider implication?

Here are some examples of change:

- Changes to the way we work (for example, during the pandemic and post-pandemic)
- People changes in the workplace
- New products or services being implemented
- Systems, process or procedural changes
- Mergers and acquisitions
- Redundancies or organisational restructuring
- Role and responsibilities changes

Now, if that same change were to happen again today, what would be different? What were some of your observations or learnings?

Again, note them down.

Feedback: Some of those differences, observations or learnings might be things that you can share feedback on within your organisation and of course, there may be some personal differences and learnings that you can take on board for yourself.

There are a lot of change models out there in the world that I like, such as Lewin's Change Management model, which covers the way we freeze and unfreeze, along with the Kubler-Ross model, originally a model on the stages we go through when we experience grief which was reworked for managing organisational change.

Once again, I'm a fan of simplicity and I'm also a fan of a nice mnemonic, so I created a model and framework that I call ***the EDGE model***.

I developed and designed this model during the first lockdown as a follow-up to the Resilient Mindset session I provided for CIPD. It's about how we EDGE toward change in four stages – consider, evaluate, question and find support.

The EDGE Model

We know that change can bring feelings of confusion, stress, overwhelm and worry for many people but change doesn't always have to imply something negative. For some people, it can also be interesting, refreshing, fun and energising.

Change can be what happens to us, around us, within us and sometimes, what we initiate to bring about change. How we respond to change can aid our management of how we work through it. As business leaders and managers, we can plan and strategise the right steps forward to enable others to adapt and work with change.

Our natural defence when change occurs can initiate our fight, flight or freeze responses but it's important not to stick your head in the sand. Learning to embrace and confront change head-on can reduce feelings of stress, alongside taking care of your body and mind whilst you are coping and going through the process of change.

It's important to decide what the time frame for change is. How you communicate change will impact you and your colleagues, either positively or negatively. Understand that change might cause hesitancy and consider how you can best support your people through change and how you will then recognise milestones.

Before we get into the EDGE model in more detail, I'd like you to consider a change that might be on the horizon or already afoot for you or your team.

Ask yourself: What is that change?

Note it down and then ask yourself the following four questions:

- What is the change and when will this happen?
- What action do you need to take to help people feel more comfortable and ready for change?
- How will you get your people involved and engaged in the change?
- What will you provide to ensure this happens as smoothly as possible?

Change can be challenging and hugely distressing for people, but it can also present opportunities too. During periods of change, it's key to update the people around you, even when there isn't anything of significance to share.

It's also important to be prepared to understand and listen to what's happening and to see what opportunities may arise, paying close attention to prepare for all scenarios – even worst-case scenarios – to see how you could minimise their impact.

Adapting to your new situation with new routines and learning from your experience of change gives you the chance to reflect and re-evaluate your existing goals or create new ones.

Change can be an emotional time, so do acknowledge your feelings but also acknowledge that you can only control your reaction to change and not the change itself.

An essential coping strategy is giving yourself time to adapt and accept change and to feel empowered by identifying your skill sets, resources, strengths and a network of support to guide you through.

The EDGE coaching model will help you to cope with the journey of change tailored to Engage, Develop, Guide and Embed successful change within your teams, communication strategy and business processes.

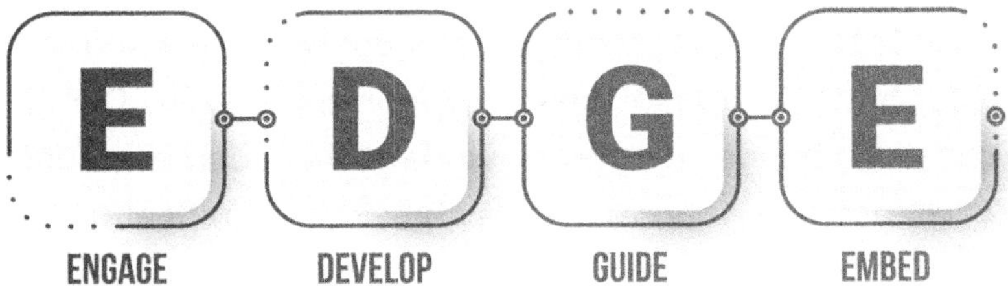

ENGAGE

In the Engage stage of the EDGE model, the focus is on building strong connections and rapport with team members to establish a foundation for change. Leaders should prioritise open communication and active listening and demonstrate genuine interest in their team members' well-being.

Ask yourself:

- How do you currently engage in conversations with your team members?
- What strategies do you employ to ensure open and active discussions?
- How do you demonstrate a genuine interest in your team member's personal and professional lives?
- Where can you listen out for both the head and heart thoughts of your team members?
- How do you currently support the well-being of your team members, both personally and professionally?

You can bring it to life by...

Initiating Helpful Conversations - Proactively initiate conversations with team members to understand their perspectives, concerns, and aspirations.

Creating Inclusive Communication Channels - Establish open communication channels where team members feel comfortable sharing their ideas, feedback and concerns.

Demonstrating Genuine Interest - Take a personal interest in each team member by actively listening to their needs, recognising their achievements and providing support where needed.

Promoting Well-being Initiatives - Implement well-being programmes and initiatives that support the physical, mental and emotional health of team members.

Leading by Example - Be the change that you want to see by actively engaging in conversations and demonstrating empathy.

DEVELOP

In the development stage, your focus should be on fostering growth and development within the team. This involves promoting new ways of working, building resilience and providing support for skill and mindset development.

Ask yourself:

- How do you encourage your team members to embrace change and new ways of working?
- What initiatives do you have in place to support the resilience and well-being of your team?
- What, if any, gaps in skill sets or mindsets are there within your team? How do you plan to support them?

- What strategies do you use to create alternative approaches when faced with challenges or obstacles?
- How do you incorporate feedback and learning into your team's development plan?

You can bring it to life by...

Fostering a Learning Culture - Encourage continuous learning and development by providing opportunities for training.

Encouraging Innovation - Create a safe environment where team members feel empowered to experiment with new ideas, approaches and technologies.

Providing Future Focused Feedback - Regularly provide feedback and support to help team members identify areas for growth and improvement.

Promoting Collaboration - Facilitate collaboration and knowledge sharing among team members to strengthen collective expertise.

Setting Clear Goals and Expectations - Work together to define clear goals, expectations and performance metrics. Coach and support your team members' development efforts and progress.

GUIDE

The Guide stage involves providing individualised support and empowerment to navigate through the change process. Leaders should focus on maintaining a steady pace, empowering their team members and ensuring they successfully navigate evolving plans.

Ask yourself:

- How do you tailor your support to individual team members' needs during times of change?
- In what ways do you empower your team members to take ownership of their roles and responsibilities?
- How do you maintain a steady pace while guiding your team through change?
- Think of a time when you successfully guided your team through an evolving plan or situation. What did you do there that worked well? How can you replicate that?
- How do you demonstrate a caring and empathetic approach while guiding your team through change?

You can bring it to life by...

Offering Individualised Support - Tailor support and guidance to meet the unique needs and preferences of each team member, considering their strengths, areas of focus and career aspirations.

Empowering Decision-Making - Empower team members to make decisions and take ownership of their work by providing autonomy, resources and support.

Maintaining Momentum - Maintain pace while guiding the team through the change process, addressing any obstacles or setbacks as they come up.

Communicating with Transparency - Keep team members informed and engaged by providing regular updates on progress, changes and upcoming milestones.

Leading with Empathy - Demonstrate empathy and compassion towards team members, acknowledging their efforts, concerns and contributions during challenging times.

EMBED

At the Embed stage, the focus shifts towards cementing the changes and ensuring they become part of the team culture and practices. This involves strengthening fair work approaches, promoting psychological safety and maintaining healthy daily routines.

Ask yourself:

- How do you ensure that fair work approaches are consistently implemented within your team?
- What steps do you take to promote psychological safety and trust among team members?
- How do you encourage teamwork and collaboration within your team?
- What strategies do you use to encourage and support the desired behaviours and practices within your team culture?

You can bring it to life by...

Committing to New Practices - Embed new behaviours, processes and practices into the team culture by consistently supporting colleagues.

Promoting Accountability - Be accountable for demonstrating organisational values, standards and expectations, fostering a sense of ownership and responsibility.

Celebrating Successes - Recognise and celebrate achievements, milestones and successes as a team.

Promoting Continuous Improvement - Encourage that mindset of continuous improvement by seeking feedback, reviewing progress and results and identifying opportunities for fine-tuning.

Underestimating Workplace Communication

Communication is such an underestimated commodity in the workplace. If organisations, along with their leaders and managers, paid even a teeny tiny amount more attention to how often they communicate, what they are communicating and the why behind the message, they would greatly influence employee engagement for the better, as well as morale and higher rates of staff retention too.

Fundamentally, communication is at the very core of our lives and business interactions. Well-structured and ordered communication can successfully aid our understanding and our positions; it says who we are as individuals and can actively assist us in how we operate.

Communication is the very backbone of all that you do within your business.

Communication has the power to boost morale, productivity, well-being and the psychological safety of your teams and colleagues.

Poor communication will inevitably lead to your team members feeling dissatisfied, with higher rates of absenteeism along with the contemplation of their future as an employee and whether they are a good fit within your business. This will undoubtedly impact their communication and effective output, which in turn, creates a toxic environment with the potential to damage your organisation's reputation, growth and development as well as that of your team, too.

As an organisation, leader or manager, when communicating with individuals in your teams, it's useful to promote:

Active listening

Empathise with your co-workers and teams. Where possible, promote daily conversations, regular one-to-ones, in-person weekly meetings, constructive and supportive feedback along with recognising great work by shining a light on those who are going the extra mile.

Inclusivity

Seek progress on projects, ask for regular updates and plan for communication, especially with those who are remote working.

Mindful Communication Delivery

Be mindful in a way that best carries your communication. Pay close attention to the way in which it's given and how the message could be taken, noting that mood and tone cannot always be easily understood from emails or texts.

Clarity of Expected Results and Outcomes

Ensure clearly focused goals and wider business objective goals are communicated well, so that everyone is aware, involved in decisions and equally driven by their contribution towards agreed solutions.

Effective and Successful Communication

Communication should always be at the business heart of how decisions, plans, strategies and change are conveyed. Ensure active and real-time conversations are encouraged with as much notice as you can offer, remembering that the best possible outcomes can be achieved through actionable steps.

Team Strength

Strong teams always communicate at their best and have the capacity to build positive and productive cultures that can overcome adverse challenges and difficult times. They can problem-solve when things go wrong or through periods of change, whether positive or negative and can work with boosted creative flow. Discovering innovative ways of working, they can showcase their skills, value and potential, all whilst feeling 'seen' within the team.

Collaboration

Bolster individuals and their teams to work together to seek resourceful and cohesive business solutions, therefore enhancing the dynamic and development of not just themselves, but the organisation too.

And lastly, even when there is nothing new to update people with, communicate anyway, even if it is just to let people know that it is still the same as before. Eliminating any worry that a person may have about what 'change' is going on in the background, which, if mismanaged, can breed speculation and distrust.

Engage, Transform and Supercharge 'Change' Summary

Engage

Support and embrace change in the workplace with open, continued communication and transparency. It's about creating a culture where team members feel informed, involved and empowered throughout any organisational change. Communicate the reasons behind the change, its expected impact and the role of each person in contributing to its success. Invite feedback, questions and any worries or concerns from colleagues, actively listening to their perspectives and insights. Involving colleagues in the change early on in the process helps to build trust, alignment and commitment, laying the foundation for a successful EDGE towards the change required.

Transform

Manage change to support and help people shift from resistance to resilience. Reframing change as an opportunity for growth, learning, and innovation, rather than a threat or disruption, can be hugely comforting. Provide support, resources, coaching, mentoring and training to help team members adapt to any new ways of working to THRIVE in the changing environment.

Supercharge

Support your people to champion change and lead by example. Foster a collaboration-based culture, breaking down any silos that might exist and encouraging diverse insights, perspectives and expertise to drive innovation and problem-solving. In supercharging our efforts, we create a culture of change in readiness, resilience and innovation that positions us for success in a rapidly changing world.

Let's Not Stop Here: keep the momentum going and refer to the EDGE Towards Change Toolkit section in your downloadable workbook. Share it with your team and use this as an action plan to work on together.

www.dnacoach.co.uk/leadersassembleworkbook

THE SELF-CARE MINDSET

12
THE SELF-CARE MINDSET

Practising Self-Care for Workplace Well-Being

As you now know, I created a series of coaching card decks during the first pandemic lockdown; one for resilience, which we covered in an earlier chapter, a team mindset card deck which covers an abundance of topics, a good few of which I have shared in this book so far, and then a self-care mindset deck.

Now, the self-care deck was, I suppose, a little ironic for me, as back then, I certainly wasn't prioritising my self-care practices, in fact, quite the opposite in some areas. I've never been a fan of a spa day, climbing mountains or having bubble baths, which is often the connotation I draw up in my mind when it comes to what self-care looks like.

I'd often seen people posting online with the hashtags #selfcaresaturday or #selfcaresunday and there they'd be, at the top of a hill, at the gym or even sporting cucumber over their eyes, covered in what looks like 'Mrs Doubtfire' style cake batter, enjoying their facial.

To me, none of that represented self-care. Self-care to me was solely about getting enough sleep. I didn't go to the gym, I drank way too much wine, I'd eat a whole lot of rubbish and I'm not a fan of miles and miles of long, sweaty walks.

A week into lockdown, I tripped on a set of shoes in the hallway (not quite paying attention to where I was going) and I broke my ankle. To cut a long story short, five weeks later, while sporting a moon boot and having had a few wines in the garden, I went to the bathroom upstairs and on the way back down misjudged my footing with the moon boot on and off I went tumbling down the stairs like ED 209 from Robocop. Lo and behold, I fractured the other ankle. I mean, if you're going to break ankles (plural), then lockdown was the time to do it as I couldn't go anywhere anyway.

During that forced pause, not only did I realise that I needed to pay more attention to looking after myself, but I also had a lot of time to ponder the lifestyle I was leading, always running about like a headless chicken. And then, of course, there was the larger-than-ever focus on well-being being played out across the globe due to COVID-19. This got me thinking about all of the things that make up a self-care mindset in its approach and routine. It's not all about mountains, facials and bubble baths. It's not just for Saturdays and Sundays, either. Self-care, in its most basic form, is important every single day and it shows up in many ways.

Tottering off down my usual rabbit hole, I started to identify many topics that can influence our self-care and well-being overall. I identified over sixty-five topics, all linked to how a person can feel fulfilled – with all of them ending in the suffix ful.

Self-care, both personally and professionally, should be seen as a well-being mindset and approach.

One of the mitigating factors in my leaving a previous job was a lack of self-care and well-being focus. I was pulled aside by my leading director and told I was in trouble because... wait for it... my team left at their finish time, every evening.

Yup. That.

How dare they? (Rolls eyes emoji)

Insert lots of swear words.

I challenged it with “And why shouldn’t they?”

I was told it didn’t demonstrate commitment (more eye-rolling, and yes that’s a microexpression or aggression but one I feel was totally warranted here).

I asked if anyone noticed that the team continuously came in early, smashed their targets, got great feedback from the client and were bloody great at their jobs.

The silence was intense.

> Every single one of us is more than our jobs.

Your contracted hours are exactly that. We shouldn't feel pressured to do more as a vanity measure or to show how committed we are.

Everyone should be able to show up, be their best, do great work, enjoy it, be treated well and then be able to go home feeling fulfilled... not depleted.

So, with that in mind, I'd like EVERY single one of you reading this book to review your own, as well as your organisations, self-care and well-being strategies. This might start with some simple conversations, but they are conversations that need to be had.

Let me share with you a flavour of some of the self-care mindset topics, their definition (some have dual meanings) and things for you to consider in being able to apply each to your life and work.

ARMFUL - *The amount that your arms can hold.*

How much should you be taking on and how much can your arms hold?

The answer lies in recognising when we say yes to too many things within the workplace or even socially, which can lead to stress and burnout.

Many resources are stretched, along with the changing landscape of work and time expectations etc., it can all be too much to juggle, which can put people at risk of feeling weighed down and unable to achieve or tipping the balance completely of being able to successfully manage them.

This is where we want to be providing support and encouragement to team members, promoting collaboration and personal growth.

We can do this by scheduling regular check-ins with team members to discuss their goals, challenges and development opportunities. Use these check-ins to offer helpful feedback and recognition to acknowledge individual achievements and facilitate and foster a culture of learning and collaboration.

Ask yourself from a professional context:

- How do you currently support the development and well-being of your team members?
- In what areas do your team members need the most support and how can you provide it effectively?
- How can you empower your team to take on new challenges and grow professionally?
- All without inadvertently leading anyone towards burnout.

For yourself personally (and of course, to coach others) ask yourself:

- How do you know you are taking on too much? What are the signs?
- How much are you currently juggling? How did you wind up with so much on your plate?
- How are you managing and balancing life and work? What will free up some time?
- How often are you saying yes to (unnecessary) things? What can you do to change this? What will allow you to manage a healthy armful?
- What will help you lift the burden of too many responsibilities? How would that feel? What can you stop, start or continue with to help?

GRATEFUL - ***Appreciative of benefits received; thankful: expressing gratitude***

What about your life and career do you appreciate and are grateful for?

One of the most powerful things you can do is to demonstrate an attitude of gratitude and have a sense of gratefulness for everything around you.

It includes being grateful for: the big things, for your health, for your family, your home but also for the simple things which can be the most effective such as everyday human kindness like when someone helps us by opening a door or a work colleague helping us with a small activity etc.

Finding joy in gratitude, being grateful and recognising and cultivating this within your teams comes by thanking people for their value, effort and the results that they bring to your organisation which in turn builds and cements confidence and trust.

Cultivate an attitude of gratitude to foster positivity, resilience, and stronger interpersonal relationships.

We can do this by starting a gratitude journal to reflect on the things you're thankful for each day. Integrate gratitude rituals into team meetings by acknowledging individual contributions and taking time to personally thank team members for their efforts and achievements.

Ask yourself from a professional context:

- What aspects of your work and life are you grateful for?
- How can you express gratitude to your team members and colleagues more frequently?
- In what ways can you shift your perspective to find gratitude in challenging situations?

For yourself personally (and, of course, to coach others) ask yourself:

- What are you grateful and thankful for today? Why are you grateful for it? How and when are you expressing your gratitude? To whom?

- What about your upbringing are you grateful for? What in nature are you grateful for? What about your career are you grateful for?
- Where is the most beautiful place you have been to?
- What do you really appreciate about your life? What do you love about your home?
- What three things do you love about your friends, family and the area you live in?

PLAYFUL - ***Full of fun and high spirits, good-natured/humoured.***

What can you do to schedule, encourage and incorporate being playful within your workplace and teams as well as your everyday life?

Commonly mistaken as only being a childlike quality, being playful is frequently used by high-performing teams as a creative and innovative tool to seek solutions and problem solve as well as a relaxant known to reduce stress.

This topic is about discovering how you can be more playful at work and home, how you can find joy in what you do and how to make that applicable as a leader within your organisation's settings and teams. It's about embracing a light-hearted and creative approach to work and life.

Ask yourself from a professional context:

- When was the last time you allowed yourself to engage in a playful activity?
- How can you infuse more playfulness into your leadership style and team interactions?
- What innovative ideas can emerge when you approach challenges with a playful mindset?

For yourself personally (and, of course, to coach others) ask yourself:

- Do you play? How do you play? When do you play? Where could you be more playful in your life? How will you become more playful?
- What could playfulness do for your personal and professional relationships?
- Where is your playground? What can you press play on today? How can you live a more playful life?
- How are you scheduling time for play? What new things and experiences can you try today?
- How can you add more play to your everyday life?

RESTFUL - ***Affording, marked by, or suggesting rest; tranquil, giving or conducive to rest.***

How can you incorporate good rest periods into your lifestyle?

This topic can come with connotations of being lazy, sedentary and not moving but it's important to highlight that being restful does not necessarily mean being still (although sleep is imperative for us to be at our best). Being restful comes from seeking tasks and activities that help you to switch off, for example, it could be reducing screen time and social media scrolling or it could be climbing mountains, spa days or having a bubble bath (all the things I don't seem to do) but for others it could be in spending quality time with family and friends, eating out, eating well, exercising or perhaps in learning something new.

It could also be about finding rest amongst our busy lives and being able to help ourselves to unwind and be restful of mind – this could be as simple as taking a seat, having some quiet time, reading a book or newspaper or even cuddling the dog. Defining restful is bespoke to each of us.

Finding what works for you could involve analysing what a restful day or evening could look like, for example, learning to say no and creating healthy boundaries to carve opportunities of time for yourself to discover what being restful is like for you.

It's about prioritising adequate rest and rejuvenation to optimise that lovely cognitive function, productivity and overall well-being. For this, you might establish a consistent sleep schedule and create a conducive sleep environment. I know I need to be well rested or that grumpy wee pigeon state I mentioned previously is the one that prevails. Encourage your team to take regular breaks throughout the day to recharge. Try practising mindfulness or meditation to quiet the mind and promote relaxation.

Ask yourself from a professional context:

- How do you currently prioritise rest in your daily work routine?
- What obstacles prevent you from getting sufficient rest and how can you overcome them?
- What relaxation techniques resonate with you and how can you incorporate them into your working day?

For yourself personally (and, of course, to coach others) ask yourself:

- How much rest and relaxation time do you have per week? When have you experienced exhaustion or burnout? What could have prevented that?
- How much sleep do you get? What is your typical sleep routine? How does your sleep environment aid a restful night?
- How do you switch off? What are you doing to unwind? What is preventing this?
- What would a restful day or evening involve for you?
- How much time are you investing in having good rest periods? How are you incorporating rest into your lifestyle?

TIMEFUL - ***Seasonable, timely, sufficiently early – consisting of and occupying time at a particular moment in time***.

How effectively are you managing your time? Are you making time for friends and family, to have a rest or to go on holiday?

Being timeful involves openly analysing how much you are taking on in order to make meaningful changes for the benefit of ourselves and our needs. It's about managing our time effectively to balance work responsibilities, personal interests, hobbies or activities.

Take a look at your diary – do you have consistent, back-to-back meetings and is your schedule preventing you from taking a break, having a cup of tea or coffee or even using the toilet facilities? When are you finding time in your calendar to complete actions that are agreed to in those back-to-back meetings?

Has time been overloaded, and could you set some healthy boundaries with others about what you would like to do and what you can realistically achieve?

Think about how you might use time-blocking techniques to allocate dedicated time for specific tasks and activities. Delegating or outsourcing non-essential tasks to free up time for high-priority activities can be super useful. And, of course, setting boundaries around work hours and commitments can protect personal time and prevent burnout.

Ask yourself from a professional context:

- How do you currently prioritise and allocate your time between work and your personal life?
- What time management strategies have been most effective for you in the past?
- In what areas do you struggle with time management, and how can you improve?

For yourself personally (and, of course, to coach others) ask yourself:

- What does your calendar currently look like? What can you move or take out? What is missing from your calendar that you recognise is important, but you have not dedicated time to?
- How are you managing your time? How effectively are you using your time?
- What could save you at least one hour a day if you stopped doing it? What should you be making time for in your life?
- How will you create the life you want and make the most of your time?
- What makes you feel that you are not in control of your own time? What can you do to reclaim it?

HUMOURFUL - ***Humorous temperament or disposition.***

What opportunities are there for laughter and humour in your everyday life? What humour can you bring to situations and events you're facing and can humour bring something to those people around you?

Life is way too short to not find joy and humour within it. Being humourful is seeking the things that you find fun and laughing at the light-hearted stuff or the embarrassing 'why me?' moments – from the ridiculous to the clumsy.

Take my two broken ankles, that's one example of a plethora of calamities I have found myself in over the years and continue to find myself in. I swear I could trip over fresh air. But I have to laugh... otherwise everything becomes too serious.

It's in trying not to take things too seriously and to create normality where thoughts can become flexible and attitudes can become adaptable.

This can be done by using humour appropriately to alleviate tension, foster camaraderie and enhance communication in the workplace. Of course, be mindful of cultural sensitivities and individual preferences when employing humour, ensuring inclusivity and respect for diverse perspectives.

Ask yourself from a professional context:

- How do you incorporate humour into your interactions and communication style at work?

- How can you use humour as a tool to build rapport, diffuse tension and strengthen relationships in both professional and personal settings?

For yourself personally (and, of course, to coach others) ask yourself:

- What opportunities are there for laughter and humour in your everyday life? What part does humour play for you?
- What funny moments can you recall from your past that fill you with joy and happiness?
- What humour can you bring to situations and events that you are facing? What can humour bring to those people around you?
- How can you look on the bright side of life? What healthy dose of humour can you have daily?
- What does laughter do for your mind, your mood and your body?

By consistently implementing and incorporating daily well-being of self and collective care practice, you can minimise burnout and reduce overwhelm within the workplace to ensure you can be at your very best by aligning your thoughts and actions in a more positive way, both in body and mind, for optimum business and personal self-care success.

Let's review with a final summary of engage, transform and supercharge.

Engage, Transform and Supercharge 'Self-Care' Summary

Engage

Promoting a self-care mindset and approach in the workplace starts with fostering a culture that values and prioritises employee well-being. It's about creating an environment where employees feel supported and encouraged to focus on their physical, mental and emotional health.

Initiate open conversations about self-care and well-being, destigmatising discussions around mental health and stress management. By engaging employees in the conversation and providing them with the support they need, we create a workplace culture where self-care isn't just the tonic for Saturdays and Sundays.

Transform

To demonstrate a self-care mindset and approach, we need to shift from reactive to proactive strategies. It's about moving beyond merely addressing symptoms of burnout or stress to fostering resilience and promoting the holistic well-being of the entire person, not just the one who shows up at work.

It's about encouraging employees to take regular breaks (I can't believe that we have to remind people about this... we are not our job title or a number), and engage in activities that promote relaxation and stress reduction.

It's about providing opportunities for flexible work arrangements, such as remote work or flexible hours, to accommodate team members' individual needs and preferences. It's promoting a work-life balance, setting clear boundaries around expectations and workload, and empowering colleagues to take ownership of their health and prioritise their overall well-being.

Supercharge

Role model as a leader by prioritising your own self-care and well-being and openly communicating about your self-care practices. You can set a positive example by taking those breaks, prioritising balance and seeking support when needed.

Let's Not Stop Here: keep the momentum going and refer to the Self-Care Mindset Toolkit section in your downloadable workbook. Share it with your team and use this as an action plan to work on together.

www.dnacoach.co.uk/leadersassembleworkbook

MY CUP OF AMBITION FOR YOU

13
MY CUP OF AMBITION FOR YOU

Final Thoughts

All of the topics I have shared in this book are the areas that I am super passionate about. It all comes down to being that good human being in the workplace and putting people at the core of everything you do.

> My cup of ambition is that our world of workplaces is filled with leaders, managers and colleagues who want to build impactful and inclusive, people-centred workspaces and environments. Fostering this is not a 'nice to have', it's a 'must' so that we enable people to thrive.

Sure, there are processes, policies and procedures you have in your organisation that should be followed but let's ensure that whatever those processes are, you are following them with a people focus.

Every single day we should be able to bring our 'whole' selves to work, safe in the knowledge that we are valued, heard and supported.

Leading and managing our organisations with a coaching approach is what will make our organisations even more successful too.

So, what does that culture look like? Everything that's in this book.

A culture where everyone is accepted and included, where every day we have curious conversations infused with a coaching approach in a psychologically safe way, strengthened by future-focused feedback, trust, integrity, self-care and a resilient growth mindset at its core.

As leaders and managers, we should be inviting people to engage and share their thoughts, ideas and concerns, actively listening to that feedback and acting on it so that we are continuing to transform the 'way we do things around here'. We should always be considering what we can do to strengthen the traits and skills that people do well at/excel within and in supporting the areas that may need to be enhanced or improved. That is how we 'supercharge', by keeping the continual building focus on bolstering our strengths.

How will you continue to be the utterly amazing person that you are in the workplace?

How will you show up at your best both personally and professionally?

All of the models and frameworks shared within this book give you some thoughts to consider and process and hopefully will spark an idea or a conversation, a change or a point from which to move forward.

We all have our unique personalities, styles and approaches – don't be afraid to let people see the entire you, not just the person who shows up at work. And remember, it's okay to be vulnerable and share any vulnerabilities with others. We are, after all, human.

You don't have to become a carbon copy of everyone else. You don't have to conform to one standard way of being. You don't have to *become* a coaching model. You don't need to be all stuffy and rigid or so corporate that you end up in pinstripe suits with shoulder pads barking orders at folk and leading the shitty committee.

Talk to people, ask questions, listen, support and look out for one another. Do great and meaningful work that matters and have fun whilst doing it.

Working nine-to-five, or whatever your core hours are, doesn't have to be a place that's all take and no give. It should totally be a place where we all thrive in an enjoyable and fulfilling workspace to make a living.

Although I do wish Dolly sang about Working ten-til-two instead. I think I'll drop her a note.

Acknowledgements

Where to begin?

It has to start and continue to be my two biggest and most loved champions, cheerleaders and entourage. Affectionately, colloquially, locally and interchangeably written, known and introduced as **Big Stevie and Wee Ruby.** Otherwise referred to as my mum and dad. My real-life heroes and greatest supporters, without whom this book would have been impossible. It is to you, the mini-celebrities that you are (possibly global now), that I dedicate this, my very first, published book.

The laughter, love and unconditional care they share are what lifts me each and every single day. To write about all of our shenanigans and all of the reasons why they mean the world to me, would need an entire book in its own right. Talking about family, history, slices of life experience, funny situations, unplanned scenarios and stories we've lived through are the memories I'll cherish and carry forward and will forever hold a special place in my heart. Maybe one day I'll have the honour of getting to write that family book.

My 'stage' name might be Royal (the joys of taking another person's surname while married – rolls eyes) but I am and always will be a McKeown, through and through. That surname revelation might be a mic drop moment for the folks who have known me professionally for a long time.

Thank you, **Big Stevie,** for your wild sense of humour and infectious laugh and for passing me copious cups of tea. I'm pretty sure I get my humorous streak (and singing voice) 'shake it off', 'let's move on' type of spirit and 'don't worry what other people will think' attitude, from you. My Big Daddio, you are an absolute legend.

For settling my panic station moments, **Wee Ruby** I have to thank you for washing your beautiful calm and logical approach over me. The unwavering, nurturing nature that you have is why I care about people – because of your gentle and loving influence on me. My Wee Mummio, you are an absolute smasher.

I'm putting out a huge megaphone shout-out to you both. Thank you for everything you do for me and Tillie. We both love you hunners.

A big, big thank you for the patience of Abigail Horne and the Authors and Co team, keeping me afloat whilst I went through my various 'I cannot do this' moments, pushing me to the finishing line. You are absolute superstars Abi, Deanne, Jo, Carol and Hazel.

To the simply wonderful Amber L Smith, you are a phenomenal wordsmith with one of the most utterly delightful personalities that I have ever come across. Your help as my beta reader and editor has been nothing short of amazing. Thank you so much. You can procure Amber's services via her website here **www.simplyamberlou.com**.

For Rob Wells and Joshua Scott, my business graphic designers – without you both, my brand would be the drawings I have sent you on my Remarkable. Could you imagine that? I can see you laughing now.

Josh, in particular for helping me bring my Coaching Card Decks to life, all of which stemmed from that personal project back in 2015, where you created Big Stevie's book cover for Travis PI (he loved that so much) and of course, for introducing me to Rob.

Rob, who has taken over that great work to help me build my business branding to where it is today, your crafting, creating and building of all the wonderful workbooks, toolkits, marketing resources and client stuff is always out of this world and utterly outstanding. Rob has produced all of the internal book graphics from the models I have created over the years too, he's a pure legend.

Thank you both.

You can connect with Joshua Scott by finding him on LinkedIn here - **https://www.linkedin.com/in/josh-scott-56a40b62/**

And to get in touch with the wonderful Rob via his freelance graphic design business **https://mintcreate.co.uk/** and on LinkedIn here **https://www.linkedin.com/in/rob-wells-5b75b312b/**

To the fabulous person that is Toni Martin and her amazing team. Thank you for assisting me with all the tech stuff in my business, which I still cannot get my head around. You've helped me through the tears, snotters and painful headache of 'tech overwhelm' to being in a position where I have a fab online presence. I take my hat off to you. You can find Toni and the team here **https://tonimartin.co/**

To all my nearest, dearest, besties, amazing friends and my rock of a family, you know who you are, and I am gratefully humbled to have 'lucked out' by having you all by my side. You have been there for me in one way or another, usually in a multitude of ways, getting me out of trouble (quite literally) with midnight drives and Pickford vans. Thank you for being the awesome human beings I talk about in this book in every aspect of life.

Karen Knight, Kevin Knight, Barbara Clark (my Bing Bong as she's known), Nicola McKeown, Rhona Vize, Lynsey Hammerman, Michelle Foy, Claire Newman, Lynne Gamble, Jonny Shand, Lucy Jacobs, Jessica Bentley-White, Sundeep Sidhu, Ben Oxford, Susan Earle/Crawford (I still can't get used to that you know), Nicky Lloyd-Greame (I promise I've spelt your surname right), Colin Lamb, Colin Wright, Katy Morrison, Vicky Connor, Gordon White, Alan and Gemma Scott, Katie Gemmell, Laura Kodur, Paul Cartwright, Christopher Sayle, Colin MacPherson, Fiona McGillivray, Big Brian and Sheena Knight, Toby and Kate McCartney, and of course all of the McKeown's and *most* of the McClymont's (if you know you know) much love to you all, what a family and a privilege to be a part of. Thank you to each and every single one of you 😊. I hope I haven't forgotten anyone, and if I have then I will allow you to stand on my toe the next time you see me.

To some newly acquired pals and business besties who have helped me progress in my business, held me as accountability partners, championed me with writing this book and kept my spirits up or who have inspired me to be my best and of course are now firm friends. Niki Hutchison, Shauleen Johnson (I wouldn't know the lovely Charlotte McCormick if it weren't for you too), Nadia Hossen, Jenny Drew and Laurie Macpherson to name a few.

Thank you also to the fantastic folks I mentioned in the body of my book right at the start, Stewart, John, Charlotte, Jess, my Tracey Smith and Alex. It was genuinely the greatest workplace (and life), and you were the best role models.

A final message of thanks to fourteen-year-old Laura (me), just after her careers advice conversation... for ignoring that shit and for going out there and absolutely smashing it!!

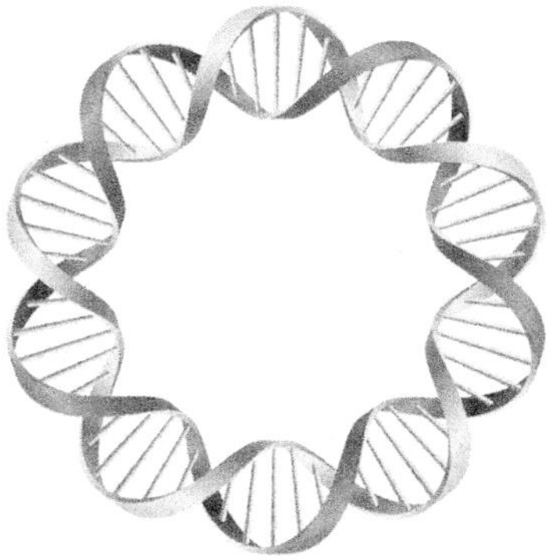

Bibliography

Clark, T. R. (2020) *The Four Stages of Psychological Safety.* ReadHowYouWant Publishing

Whitmore, J. (2017). *Coaching for Performance: The Principles and Practices of Coaching and Leadership (5th ed.).* Nicholas Brealey Publishing.

Schein, E. H. (1980). *Organizational Culture and Leadership.* Jossey-Bass.

Lewin, K. (1948). *Resolving Social Conflicts.* American Psychological Association.

Edmondson, A. (2018). *The Fearless Organization: Creating Psychological Safety in the Workplace for Learning, Innovation, and Growth.* Harvard Business School.

Ibarra, H & Scoular, A (2019) *The Leader as Coach.* Harvard Business Review https://hbr.org/2019/11/the-leader-as-coach

Goleman, D. (1996). *Emotional Intelligence: Why It Can Matter More Than IQ.* Bloomsbury Paperbacks.

Bradberry, T., & Greaves, J. (2009). *Emotional Intelligence 2.0.* Talent Smart.

Maxwell, J. C. (1998). *The 21 Irrefutable Laws of Leadership: Follow Them and People Will Follow You.* Thomas Nelson.

Williamson, J. (2021). *The Shitty Committee: A Guide to Overcoming Negative Self-Talk, Limiting Beliefs, and Self-Sabotage.* Self-Published.

Clear, J. (2018). *Atomic Habits: An Easy & Proven Way to Build Good Habits & Break Bad Ones.* Random House.

Dweck, C. (2017). *Mindset: The New Psychology of Success.* Robinson.

Each coaching card set contains everything you need to develop your own mindset or to coach others. Our easy-to-use coaching card decks can be used to develop your own or your team's mindsets.

Build a **Resilient Mindset** and tackle all challenges head-on.

Develop a **Self-Care Mindset** to help recognise burn-out, improve wellbeing, and heighten mood.

Build or encourage a **Team Mindset** to make collaboration more effective than ever.

Whichever mindset suits your goals, use our coaching cards to begin developing it today.

INTRODUCING THE COACHES & LEADERS ASSEMBLE CPD MEMBERSHIP

- Accredited CPD Training
- Weekly and Monthly Zoom Sessions
- Exclusive Access to HR and Co-Coaching Clinics
- Curated CPD Learning Pathways
- Industry-Leading Guest Speaker Sessions
- Interactive Workshops and Masterclasses
- Ongoing Support and Resources
- Networking and Community
- And much more

JOIN NOW FROM £49+VAT PER MONTH

WITH DISCOUNT FOR 12 MONTHS MEMBERSHIP

WWW.DNACOACH.CO.UK/CPDMEMBERSHIP

At DNA Coach we are a registered CMI Centre and accredited coach training provider via the Association for Coaching.

We provide Leadership and Coaching qualifications through both these globally recognised accredited bodies – head on over to **www.dnacoach.co.uk** to find out more.

Like to listen to a Podcast? Then head on over to **www.dnacoach.co.uk/podcast** to listen to my very own Coaches and Leaders Assemble Podcast – the Podcast for all things Coaching, Leadership, People and Culture. Or search for 'Coaches and Leaders Assemble' wherever you consume your podcast content.

You can also view some of Laura's speaking adventures here - **www.dnacoach.co.uk/speaking** - where you can also find information on Laura's keynotes and how to book her as a speaker for your event, conference or podcast.

Printed in Great Britain
by Amazon

46802911R00158